THE BEST OF retail advertising design

THE BEST OF retail advertising design

by The National Retail Merchants Association
and the Editors of PBC, International

Distributor to the book trade in the United States:
Rizzoli International Publications Inc.
597 Fifth Avenue
New York, NY 10017

Distributor to the art trade in the United States:
Letraset USA
40 Eisenhower Drive
Paramus, NJ 07653

Distributor in Canada:
Letraset Canada Limited
555 Alden Road
Markham, Ontario L3R 3L5, Canada

Distributed throughout the rest of the world by:
Hearst Books International
105 Madison Avenue
New York, NY 10016

PBC INTERNATIONAL, INC.
One School Street,
Glen Cove, NY 11542

Library of Congress Cataloging-in-Publication Data

The Best of retail advertising design.

Includes index.
1. Advertising—United States—Awards.   2. Advertising,
Newspaper—United States—Awards.   I. National Retail
Merchants Association.   II. PBC International.
HF5816.B47   1988   659.1'0797   87-43301
ISBN 0-86636-060-3

Color separtion, printing, and binding by
Toppan Printing Co. (H.K.) Ltd. Hong Kong
Typography JW Graphics, Inc.
Photography by Justin Chu

PRINTED IN HONG KONG
10 9 8 7 6 5 4 3 2 1

Staff

Managing Director	*Penny Sibal-Samonte*
Creative Director	*Richard Liu*
Associate Art Director	*Daniel Kouw*
Editorial/Production Director	*Kevin Clark*
Project Editor	*Peter Venezia*
Artists	*Kim McCormick*
	Donna Patterson
	Bill Mack
	Allison Butlien
	Stacey Levy
Comptroller	*Pamela McCormick*

contents

PART I   FASHIONS

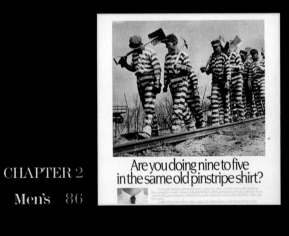

foreword

As the leader in the exchange of information about retailing, a goal of the National Retail Merchants Association is to present new information to the retail community through the publication of books, journals and other literature. *Retail Advertising Design—NoRMA Award Winners 1984–1987* is the latest NRMA publication retailers can refer to when trying to enhance the quality of their advertising.

In this book, NRMA has gathered a collection of outstanding retail newspaper advertisements, in various categories, that have won NoRMA Awards for excellence over the past four years. These ads capture the creativity and imagination that lure and hold a reader's attention.

The print media can be a most effective form of sales promotion for the retailer. It is the medium where a store's image can be presented consistently and the attention of the customer held the longest. The message is repetitious, presented to each person who picks up the newspaper or magazine.

Retail Advertising Design offers the reader an opportunity to study the technique, style and methods of recent successful ads, which will help all retailers in their pursuit of outstanding, attention-getting print advertising. Use this book to discover how you can create your own award-winning ads!

JAMES R. WILLIAMS
President, NRMA

introduction

Today's retail industry is more competitive than ever before. Retailers are not only battling their direct competitors for the attention of a potential customer, but also, the onslaught from every form of the media. In today's market, simply advertising your product's benefits or virtues is no longer sufficient. Potential customers must be amused, fascinated or entertained in an attempt to catch and hold their attention.

The National Retail Merchants Association in conjunction with the Newspaper Advertising Bureau holds an annual competition to honor the most distinguished advertisements in newspapers. These advertisements are the best presentations in a variety of categories including: merchandise ads, color ads, institutional ads, public service ads, store volume, and much more.

The key to a great advertisement is to recognize the ad's limitations. Not only the physical, graphic limitations but the psychological limitations as well. Would humor be appropriate? Should a graphic appeal be used, or maybe a comparison to a direct competitor? The theme or concept of the ad must satisfy its audience. Will the recipient be bored with a reinforcement ad? Is a product display old and played out? Perhaps a new concept or new product idea should be introduced. The advertisement must present the product or image to the recipient in a clear, concise manner. This is not to say that a variety of techniques or gimmicks cannot be employed, but remember, the primary function of the ad is to present the product.

PART I
FASHIONS

Brandstand

Creeds

Midwest Vision Centers

Rich's Elder-Beerman

Waldoff's

IKEA

Winners Apparel, Ltd.

Magasin du Nord

Hubert W. White

Holt Renfrew & Co., Ltd.

Allen Furniture

Glik's Creeds

Hubert W. White The Chesterfield Shop Ltd.

Mayor's Jewelers

ZCMI

H.A. & E. Smith

Crowley's

Haugland's Kids

John Wanamaker

Sanger Harris

Waldoff's Valley View Mall

Godchaux/Maison Blanche Jordan Marsh

Neiman Marcus

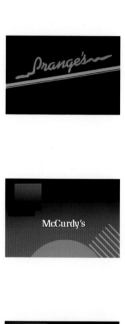

Chapter One

women's

Contemporary women's fashions are more complex than ever before. Women's changing roles in society have created a new and more straightforward approach in fashion advertising. Whether a working mother, homemaker, or executive, today's woman is not just a pretty face.

Glamour and femininity must be accompanied by competitive prices, superior quality and greater availability. Clothing must be functional as well as beautiful. Accessories must be practical as well as fashionable; new and exciting trends must be maintained. The advertising of women's wear must be direct, accurate and interesting and sustain a level of plausibility to maintain credibility in the customer's mind. The models and clothing must imitate the runways of Paris, Rome and London while simultaneously be adaptable to the sidewalks of New York, Dallas and Des Moines.

Store: Elder Beerman
Award Category: Special Award of
◄   Merit

This filmstrip featured ad from
Elder Beerman clearly displays the
colors, styles, and prices of some
affordable junior knitwear.

Store: Heritage House
Award Category: Second — $25-50
                    million

Wealth and confidence are portrayed in this Heritage House ad
announcing the opening of a new
store. The antique automobile and
relaxed pose stress the snob appeal
of this ad.

Heritage House is now at Masonville Place.

If you like your fashion classic but contemporary and cherish beautiful clothes, then you'll want to experience the
natural charm of Heritage House, opening at Masonville Place on Wednesday, August 21.

Introducing our exclusive new Heritage House tartan in pure wool. Choose either the long bias-cut skirt, as shown, $125, or a traditional pleated kilt, $110. Toss the matching shawl, $60, over a wool crepe big shirt, $98.

HERITAGE HOUSE 90

Masonville Place

Store: Saks Fifth Avenue
Award Category: Second — Silver
Merchandise Over $250
million

Leather gloves, accessories, shoes,
skirts, and outerwear are chicly displayed in this black-and-white ad
for Saks Fifth Avenue.

opposites attract

Take a second look at opposites and the
dynamics of attraction. There's plain and fancy.
Restraint and seduction. Calm and stormy.
Mr. and Ms. The list is endless. And this
season, the attraction between any two builds
to an irresistible conclusion.

In **Nomine's** sinuous scroll-shouldered cotton sweaterdress takes a very cool you and
makes you even hotter-than-hot in red. Sizes S,M,L. **$98.** Contemporary Sportswear,
mall level, JM Warwick and as noted.

This is the place!

jordan marsh

JM Boston, Braintree, Burlington, Framingham, Peabody, MA and Warwick, RI only. D-1442.

Store: Jordan Marsh
Award Category: Merit — Newspaper

Jordan Marsh portrays this red
sweater dress ad as an example of
the power of dynamic attraction.
The bold type and positive and
negative format strengthen the
copy's appeal to combining
contrasts.

MARSHALL FIELD'S PRESENTS 12 GREAT PAGES OF CAREER CLOTHING

Imagine. After all these years, they're finally following you into a meeting instead of just holding the door open. JH Collectibles projects the sense of commanding confidence you've earned along the way.

- BUSINESS PROPOSALS FOR NEW CORPORATE IMAGES

- SUCCESS DRESSING '86: THE NEW SOFTNESS

- SUITS BY DESIGN AND SUITABLE SEPARATES: PERFECT OFFICE OPTIONS

- PRIORITIES OF PROPORTION: THE COMPLETE PETITE

- OUTSIDE ORGANIZATION: COATS WITH CLOUT

- THE NEW MBA'S MANDATORY BUSINESS ACCESSORIES

NETWORK
FOR • CAREER • DRESSING

Marshall Field's

Store: Marshall Field's

Award Category: Merit — Newspaper Inserts

Network dressing from Marshall Field's launched the "dress for success" female executive fashions in this information-bulleted ad. The advertisement portrays the successful woman of today dressed in a no-nonsense, yet fashionable way.

Store: Rich's
Award Category: Special Award of Merit

Rich's saluted the beauty, glory, and tradition of France in this far from traditional angle of Parisian landmarks.

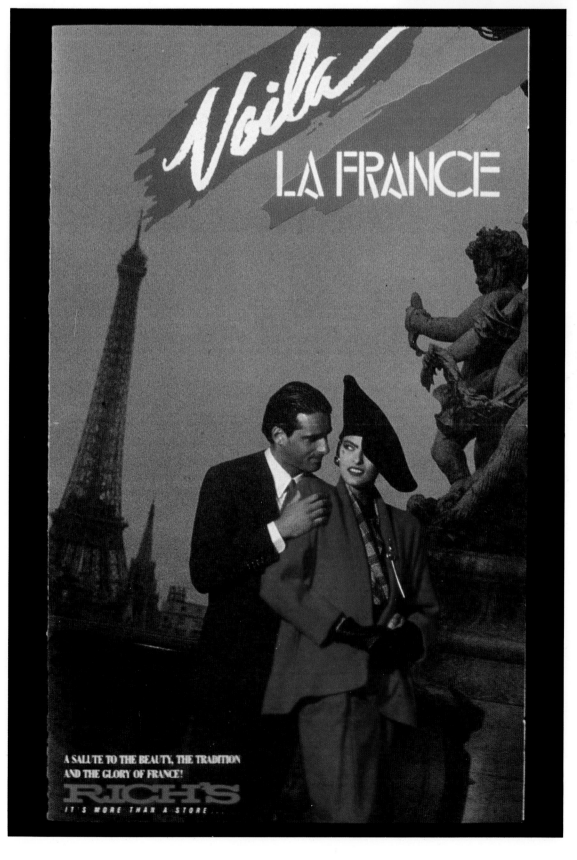

Store: B. Altman
Award Category: Merit — Newspaper
                    Inserts

B. Altman employed a positive reinforcement tactic in its Images
campaign. The ad creates a self-
assured, good feeling appeal to its
customers.

Store: Nordstrom's
Award Category: First — Newspaper

Nordstrom's illustrative ad sharply captures the style of Donna Karan's fashions in this asymmetrical/granite backdrop ad.

Store: Bullock's
Award Category: First — Gold ROP Color
Over $250 million

Bullock's offers elegant pouf-skirted
eveningwear and new mini-skirted
suits in these colorful advertisements. The centered "B" headlines
each ad, reminding the reader that
fashionable dressing is at Bullock's.

Store: Bloomingdale's
Award Category: Second — Best
Institutional
Newspaper ▶

Bloomingdale's employed high fashion sketches in charcoal tones to
proclaim their new look of Donna
Karan fashions in 1985.

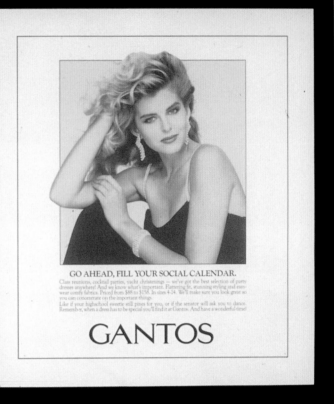

Store: Gantos

Award Category: First — Gold
Merchandise Ads Stores
$100-250 million

Gantos utilized this "Clint East-wood" dare technique to allow the customer to remove any concern she may have about finding the proper eveningwear for "that special function." Gantos wanted to portray the concept that they had a large selection of eveningwear rather than displaying merely one or two samples.

Store: The Boston Store
Award Category: Second — Silver ROP
Color $250 million

Fashion illustrations reminiscent of an artist's notebook display the new fall minis, whether slim and professional or full and fun, these skirts are available at the Boston Store.

Store: Potpourri Designs
Award Category: Merit — ROP Color
                         Stores Under $5 million

Potpourri Designs employs a "slice of life" photograph to clearly establish the audience for their line of Ellen Tracy sportswear — the working woman who wants comfortable, fashionable clothing that lends itself to her glamorous side.

Store: C.T. Crew, Greenville, North Carolina
Award Category: Not available

C.T. Crew's ad displays their new fall 1987 knits offering everything from monochromatic gray ensembles to hot primary colors in skirts and sweaters.

Store: Bullock's
Award Category: First — Gold ROP Color
Over $250 million

Unique and colorful dinnerware
alongside unique and colorful office
apparel is available at Bullock's —
as demonstrated by these large display ads.

Store: Waldoff's
Award Category: Merit — Newspaper

The snob appeal in this ad is reinforced by the photographic
excellence of these traditional
women's coordinates.

"My tastes are very simple...I only like the best."

WALDOFF'S

Store: Miller's

Award Category: Merit — ROP Color
$100-250 million

Liz Claiborne's "Antique" corduroy shirt and skirt and "Out of the Blues" pants and sweaters create a western theme for this ad. The headline satirically recalls two great moments in history — the *Gold Rush* and the *Fall of the Roman Empire*.

Store: Waldoff's
Award Category: Merit — Institutional

Waldoff's back-to-school ad complete
with Yamaha scooter appeals to
juniors who want to look good while
having fun. The summer nautical
wear ad combines comfort and style
in a bright, colorful photograph.

Store: Marshall Fields
Award Category: Second — Silver ROP
Over $250 million

Top designers' swimsuits, a deep-blue sea background, and the American Airlines logo create a vacationlike setting for this Marshall Fields ad.

Store: Donaldson's
Award Category: First — Gold Inserts
                    $100-250 million

The great outdoors, American land-
scapes and fashionable clothing
enhance these natural setting
photographic ads for Donaldson's.

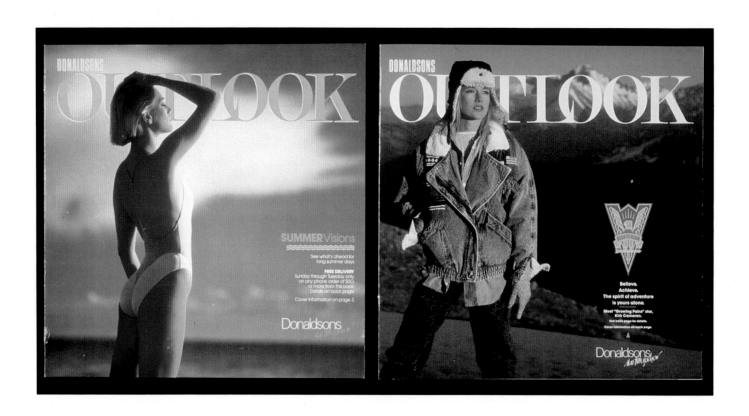

Store: Bullock's

Award Category: Second — Silver Campaigns Over $250 million

Bullock's rises to new heights in these mini skirt ads showing a variety of fabrics — wools, denims, tweeds, and stretchy knits. Leggy sketches and brief ad descriptions enhance the "short" theme presented.

Attitude. Edwin ice washed 5-pocket mini, 50.00, in Emphasis. Fun U.S.A. ice washed high-waisted, belted mini, 58.00. Area Code ice washed knit stretch mini, 65.00. Switch ice washed ruffled tiered mini, 52.00. These are found in Young

Store: Trimingham's
Award Category: Second — Silver Campaigns $5-25 million

Trimingham's sets the pace with this horizontal film strip layout advertisement. Trimingham's offers fashionable apparel for the chic cosmopolitanite to the romantic country dresser.

Store: Auer's
Award Category: Merit — Merchandise Ads Stores Under $5 million
◄

Auer's employed a hi-tech theme for their Escada evening dresses. Bright colors, asymmetrical shapes and the use of a black background and white type create a new-wave sensation to this illustrated ad.

Store: Thalhimer's
Award Category: First — Stores over
                    $100 million

Fascinating historical women are
praised in this salute to the Virginia
Museum of Fine Arts. Thalhimer's
honors America's heroines from
Pocohontas to the beaded-gown
ladies of the '80s.

Store: Robinson's
Award Category: Merit — ROP Color
Over $250 million

Pastels by Liz Claiborne are grace-
fully displayed, endorsing a myriad
of colors, available in petite sizes. A
soft yellow hue, a flaxen-haired
model, and clean, clear photography
unite to create the soft, relaxed
feeling of this ad.

Store: Leggett's
Award Category: Merit — Best Institutional Newspaper
◄

David Hechter's dinnerware, organically-grown juniors wear, and Villeroy and Boch china are all displayed in these STAR-tling merchandise ads for Leggett's.

Store: Raleigh's
Award Category: First — Gold ROP Color $50-100 million

Cotton skirts and campshirts explode in a burst of color in this fun ad. The silhouetted models positioned against a white background, allow the colors of their outfits to jump off the page.

Store: Holt-Renfrew and Co.

Award Category: First — $50-100 million

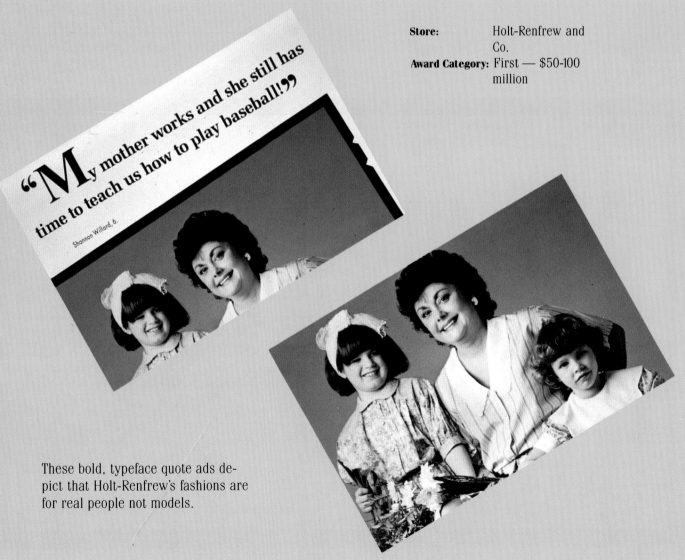

These bold, typeface quote ads depict that Holt-Renfrew's fashions are for real people not models.

Store: Goodman/Manteau
Award Category: First — $25-50 million

These fur-accessorized fashion statements promoted Goodman/Manteau's chic winter outerwear. The merchandise receives further emphasis from the stacked design of the ad: narrow centered copy placed above a large black and white photograph centered over Goodman/Manteau's logotype.

LIZ CLAIBORNE

Lightening strikes, white on white from our holiday collection of underplayed elegance by LIZ CLAIBORNE. Luxe tailored trousers, alluringly feminine in worsted wool crepe, fully lined, $85. The perfect pleated blouse to own now in poly soie de chine, $47. Completed by a lambswool-angora blend elongated cardigan with padded shoulders, $78. Trousers and blouse in sizes 4-14, sweater in sizes Small, Medium, Large. D159 Facesetter.

CAIN·SLOAN
A UNIT OF ALLIED STORES

Store: Cain Sloan
Award Category: Merit — $50-100 million

CAROLE LITTLE SCENERY

Newest directions for your summer itinerary, scenic prints of the Mediterranean from CAROLE LITTLE FOR SAINT TROPEZ WEST. Natural linen sweaters and sheer cotton-linen skirts are painted with whimsical vistas from Europe's great playground. Sweaters, $68, and matching skirts, $56. There's so much more in our CAROLE LITTLE collection of silks, cottons and rayons, $38-$98. At Green Hills, Rivergate and Hickory Hollow. D159 Pacesetter.

CAIN·SLOAN
A UNIT OF ALLIED STORES

Use your Cain Sloan Charge, American Express or Diners Club. Hickory Hollow. Green Hills and Rivergate open 10 'til 9. Downtown 10 'til 5:30. free parking with $15 purchase.

CAROLE LITTLE SCENERY

Carole Little's scenic prints of the Mediterranean are stressed in this Cain Sloan ad. A comfortable, yet well-dressed warm weather style is shown.

Store: Creeds
Award Category: Merit — Stores
                    $5-25 million

Creeds retro-glamour appeal ad highlights the trendy appeal to today's fashion-conscious woman. The white background offsets the dazzling fur coat.
Sensuality and snob appeal fortify this Creeds ad.

Store: Winners
Award Category: Merit — Stores
Under $5 million

Winners' stone-washed denims, leather pants, and designer separates at affordable prices, promoted Winners as a reasonable fashion center. The banner headline, abundant white space, and silhouetted photographs add up to a clean, straightforward ad.

Store: Glik's
Award Category: Merit — Stores
                    $5-25 million

Guess jeans for juniors were under-
statedly demonstrated in this
photographic ad for Glik's. The
muted colors and out-of-focus backdrop add to the subtleness of this ad.

Store: Dayton's

Award Category: Merit — Merchandise
Ads Over $250 million

Dayton's playfully displays the versatility of Guess' denim mini skirt; whether dressed up or down, the mini is high on the fashion charts.

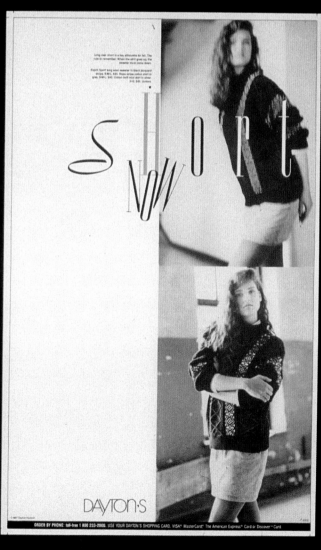

I want to make my presence felt.

BARNEYS NEW YORK

T hink slink.

BARNEYS NEW YORK

Store: Barney's

Award Category: First — Gold
Merchandise Ads
$50-100 million

Simplicity and glamour highlight
Barney's women's eveningwear and
fur ads — announcing that Barney's
is no longer a store for men only.

Store: Nordstrom's
Award Category: Second — Stores over $100 million

These fashion sketched ads accentuate Nordstrom's "first class" approach to contemporary fashion. The black and white drawings perform equally well for many forms of apparel. Elegance is emphasized through the use of contrasting black and white.

Store: Woodward's

Award Category: Merit — Stores over $100 million

Woodward's magazine approach to these ads is extremely effective through the use of large four-color photographs dealing with a single subject. Notice large display type evokes an emotional response to the picture appearing in that particular ad.

Store: ZCMI

Award Category: Merit — Merchandise
Ads $100-250 million

Leather skirts, accessories and handbags enhance this silhouetted collage ad. The stylish apparel and catchy headlines allure and alert the fashion-conscious consumer.

Store: Sanger Harris
Award Category: Merit — Stores over
$100 million

Traditional tweeds and knits highlight this women's clothing ad.

Store: Sanger Harris
Award Category: Merit — Stores over $100 million

Sanger Harris ads display chic, stylish clothing in colorful settings. This yellow cotton shirt dress is eye catching and trendy.

Store: Auer's
Award Category: Merit — Under $5 million

Anne Klein's leather boots complement Auer's fur sale in these sketch book style ads. White space and strategically placed shadowing create a realistic photographic-like approach.

YOU'VE ALWAYS THOUGHT ITALIAN MEN HAD A WAY WITH WOMEN.

Now let Valentino show you how right you are

Let us introduce the Valentino Miss V Collection. From Italy ... where style is a way of life ... comes a collection to enhance your wardrobe and your lifestyle. Clean, uncluttered lines are Valentino's signature, romanced here with the luxurious touch of black velvet. A suit that's unlike any you've worn before. The square-cut jacket makes news with its shorter length. The soft dirndl skirt commands attention in a graphic check plaid. Both pieces in wool flannel of charcoal gray—the season's most popular neutral. It's a look you'll wear with confidence from a morning meeting to an afternoon luncheon appointment. The perfect way to add Italian style to your wardrobe. Come see the Miss V Collection at Thalhimers—where it's fall for you ... and we have it all for you. French Room, Downtown.

FALL *for you*

Store: Thalhimer's
Award Category: Merit — Over $250 million

This ad featured a sketch for Valentino clothing for women who appreciate fine fashion. The top of the ad was devoted to describing several designers brand merchandise that Thalhimer's carries.

Thalhimer's featured a sketch of Anne Klein II and a brief outline of several designers in this eye-catching advertisement.

Store: Macy's
Award Category: Merit — Stores over
                    $100 million

This Prince look-alike creates a rock
star theme for these revolutionary
bubble gum stretch cotton jeans.

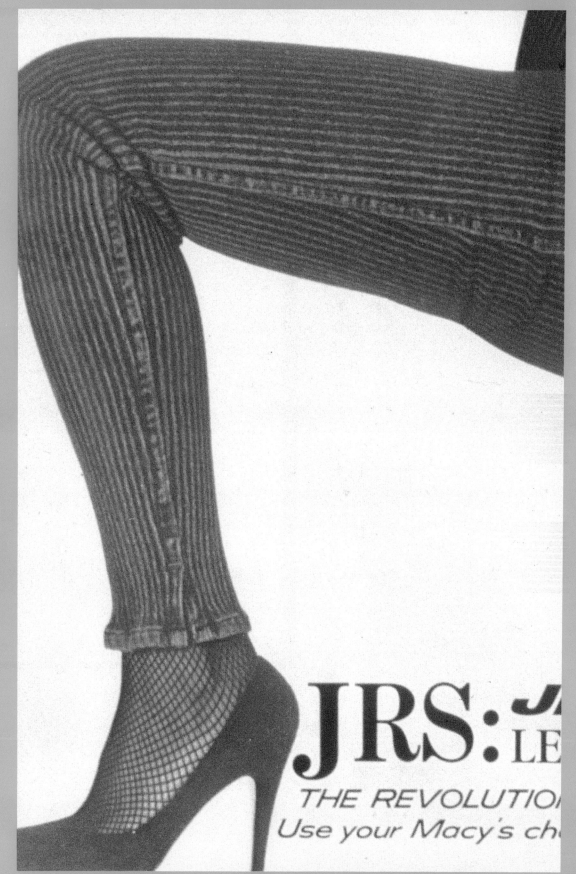

JRS: J
LE
THE REVOLUTION
Use your Macy's ch

Store: Bullock's

Award Category: First — Full Page Newspaper

Bullock's employed these bright four-color photographic full page ads to invite the customer in to a taste of the exciting world of today's designer fashions.

Store: Gantos
Award Category: Merit — $50-100 million

Gantos street chic ad emphasized a stylish, relaxed approach to casual fashions. Jeans and a plaid shirt depict a Saturday-afternoon atmosphere.
Calvin Klein's undershirts are Gantos answer to uncomfortable summertime weather.

Store: Macy's
Award Category: Merit — Over $250 million

A return to romanticism in formal wear is stressed by this prom dress advertisement.

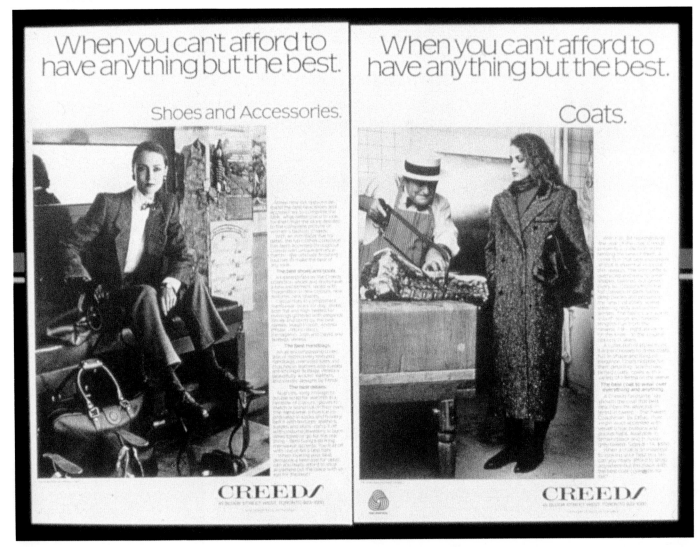

Store: Creeds
Award Category: First — Gold

Creeds accessory and winter outerwear ads emphasizes Creeds as a
source of quality merchandise. The
fine tweeds and leather goods
exemplify classic, tasteful fashions.

Store: ZCMI
Award Category: First — $100-250
million　　　►

Beaded sweater dressing was the
overall concept behind this mon-
tage of women's fashion ads.

Store: Crowley's
Award Category: Merit — $50-100 million

Crowley's women's fashionwear ads play up the warmth of fashionable dressing in coordination with Michigan living.

ZCMI saluted the "celebration of marriage" with this bridal advertisement.

LIPTON'S

Fanfare! A dress by Eklektic that definitely accentuates the positive. Images of oriental fans scatter over fine crepe de faille. A sensational dress with softly flowing sleeves, dropped waistline and the magnetic impact of a hip clinging sash. In red or blue with white fan print, sizes 2 to 12, $150. Use your Lipton's Charge Card to accentuate the positive.

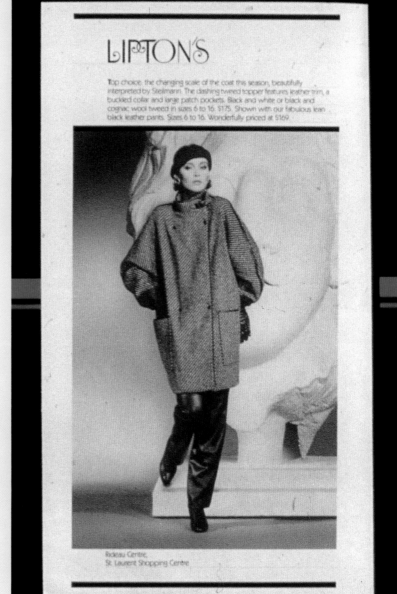

Store: Lipton's
Award Category: First — $25-50 million

Lipton's used this ad not only to promote this tweed jacket, but also to highlight their coordinating leather pants. The fan-patterned dress ad stresses the positive, confident image of this hip-sashed dress.

Store: B. Altman's
Award Category: First — $100-250 million

Westernwear never looked as wild as it does in bright colors and fine fabrics from Altman's casual selections.

INSPIRATION: AMERICA

ALTMAN'S ★

Come get a glimpse of the fabulous future,
a glance at our glorious past.

You'll want to put on the glitz with Oleg Cassini's dramatic new glitter tops. <u>Left:</u> The sequined "waterfall" blouse in sizes S,M,L. <u>280.00</u> The skirt is black, silk crepe-de-chine. Sizes 4-14. <u>88.00</u> <u>Right:</u> Scoop-neck blouse with web beaded detailing. S,M,L. <u>158.00</u> The pants are black silk crepe-de-chine. 4-14. <u>88.00</u>

Store: Raleigh's
Award Category: First — $50-100 million

Raleigh's women's eveningwear ad clearly states in bold type the objective of these gowns.

Store: Robinson's
Award Category: Merit — $100-250 million

Robinson's used this striking ad to advertise top name labels in designer swimwear that they have available at discounted prices.

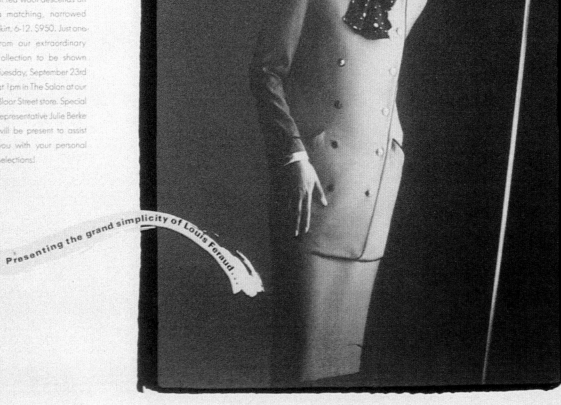

Sense the sophistication of wearing LOUIS FÉRAUD's splendid ensemble dressing! Double-breasted column of red wool descends on a matching, narrowed skirt. 6-12. $950. Just one from our extraordinary collection to be shown Tuesday, September 23rd at 1pm in The Salon at our Bloor Street store. Special representative Julie Berke will be present to assist you with your personal selections!

Presenting the grand simplicity of Louis Feraud...

HOLT RENFREW *First!*

Store: Holt Renfrew and Co.
Award Category: Merit — $100-250 million

A simplistic approach is used to display and announce the showing of Louis Ferand fashions.

Store: Frederick and Nelson

Award Category: Second — $100-250 million

This vogue advertisement demonstrates the attractive fashions for today's confident woman at Frederick and Nelson's.

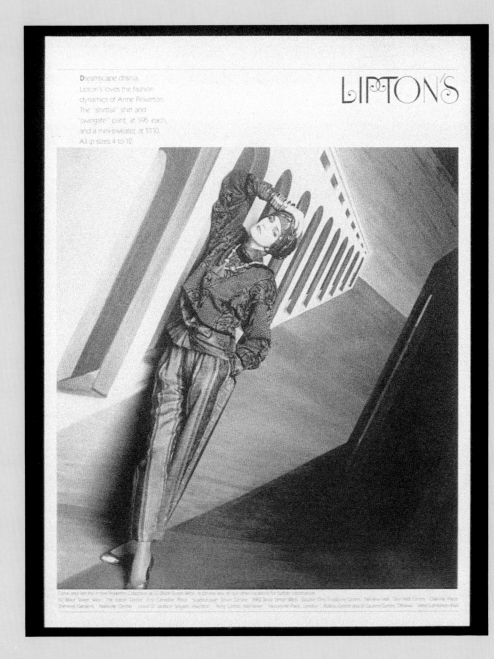

Store: Lipton's
Award Category: Second — $25-50 million

Lipton's ad featured a backless black velvet gown by Deborah Kulmer to emphasize their appeal to femininity and style.
Anne Pinkerton's fashions were dramatically displayed against an assymmetrical backdrop in this ad.

Store: Banana Republic
Award Category: First — Gold
Campaigns Stores
◄ $100-250 million

Banana Republic sells history, romance, and adventure of travel along with their functional clothing. References to the clothing were intentionally indirect, yet stress the convenience of traveling with Banana Republic clothes.

Store: Prange's
Award/Category: Merit — Stores over
$100 million

Prange's down coat ad appeals to the budget-conscious consumer in a clear practical manner.

Store: Neiman Marcus
Award Category: First — Best Institutional Newspaper

Neiman Marcus' catchy illustrations in these banner headlined advertisements launched a storewide campaign in the Fall of 1985. Cosmetics, fashions, and activewear were all united in this promotion's salute to "France by the sea."

Chapter Two
men's

Today, the popularity of fashionable clothing for men has grown by leaps and bounds. Today, menswear consists of designer labels, European styling and innovative trends and themes.

Television shows, movies and public figures all have a great influence on the men's fashion industry. Many men live alone and therefore are shopping for themselves. Whether wearing a custom-made European cut suit or merely a pair of jeans, today's fashions offer greater opportunity for men to follow their own style.

Contemporary advertising must present itself to these men in a unique, interesting manner. Men's ads must be geared toward men not merely women who shop for them. Whether appearing in the boardroom or the locker room, today's men must receive the benefits of the fashions available to them.

THE COUNTRY SIDE

SALUTING THE UNITED KINGDOM ·   12 OCTOBER – 25 DECEMBER 1987

of Britain

ZCMI

Store: ZCMI
Award Category: Second — Silver
                    Campaigns $100-250
                    million

ZCMI salutes the stylish dressing of
the United Kingdom in these British
countryside advertisements. Sweaters, tweeds, skirts, socks, caps and
colognes bring the best of England
to the United States.

Store: Jos. A. Bank Clothiers
Award Category: Merit — Merchandise
                    $50-100 million

Jos. A. Bank's offers stylish dressing
for the office and the countryside.
The professionally-dressed sales
staff creates a visual impact on the
reader and reinforces the "Business
Never Looked Better" theme.

Store: Bullock's
Award Category: Merit — Merchandise
                    Over $250 million

Bullock's displays a Giorgio Armani
suit and bright feminine prints in
these fashionable ads.

We'll Make You Look Great Even When You're Having An Off Day.

Our Sales Figures Are Some Of The Best In The Business.

Store: Raleigh's
Award Category: Merit — Campaigns $50-100 million

Colorful, comfortable robes for Father's Day are shown in Raleigh's "display of Dads" advertisement. Gone are the days of dull flannel robes, replaced by bright colors and new fabrics in men's loungewear.

FOR ALL YOU DO, DAD, THIS ROBE'S FOR YOU!

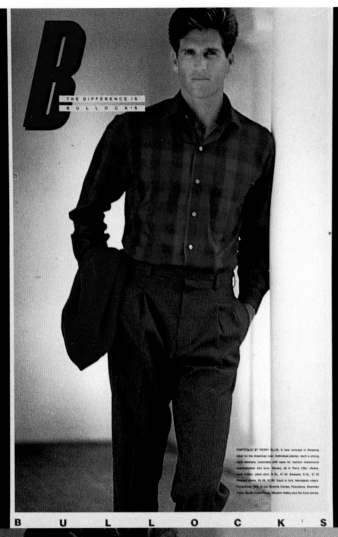

Store: Bullock's
Award Category: First — Full Page
                    Newspaper

Bullock's employed these bright
four-color photographic full page
ads to invite the customer in to a
taste of the exciting world of today's
designer fashions.

Store: Marshall Fields
Award Category: Second — Silver ROP
Color Over $250 million

Large pictorials and juxtaposed torn strips of paper give this ad powerful graphic impact. Stylish dressing is available for the traditionalist, as well as the rebel.

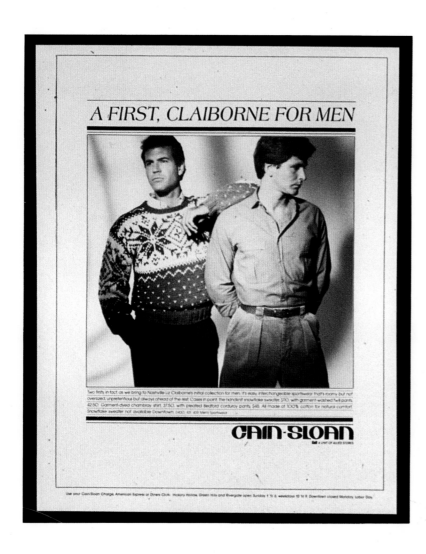

Store: Cain Sloan
Award Category: Merit — $50-100 million

Cain Sloan's menswear ads evoke the introduction of a well-known woman's fashion designer branching out into the menswear market — Liz Claiborne.

Store: Mark's Work Wearhouse

Award Category: Second — Silver Campaigns $100-250 million

Mark's Work Wearhouse offers a durable, reasonably-priced jacket available in a rainbow of colors; the perfect solution to Christmas gift problems.

Store: Hubert W. White

Award Category: Merit — Stores
Under $5 million

Value is stressed in this satirical ad
on Scottish thriftiness.

Just because you're frugal doesn't mean you have to dress like a sissy.

Twice a year like clockwork, canny bargain hunters flock to Hubert W. White. And July 9, the start of our Semi-Annual Sale, is this season's red letter day.

Fact is, most everything at Hubert W. White is sale priced. So, if in the past, you've quietly chuckled over what appeared to be an absolute steal at one of our sales, we cordially invite you back for more. And, if you have yet to set foot inside Hubert W. White, just imagine the multitude of bargains you'll come away with, practically scot-free.

Semi-Annual Sale, July 9–19

Hubert W. White

FINE APPAREL FOR MEN AND WOMEN

Store: Jos. A. Bank Clothiers

Award Category: Merit — Campaign
$50-100 million

These newspaper-styled ads endorse the pleasures of shopping and quality at Jos. A. Bank Clothiers.

Store: Raleigh's
Award Category: Second —
Newspaper

Colorful silk neckwear embellish this ad for men's accessories.

Store: Raleigh's
Award Category: First — $50-100 million

An appeal to the classics is portrayed by this sketch ad for Raleigh's menswear.

Store: Twenty-four
Award Category: First — Best Theme in Retail Advertisement

Twenty-four man encompassed several aspects of a man's wardrobe with these style-oriented ads. The "Be Your Best" message is emphasized through the use of successful local Miami businessmen, not models, in these pictorial ads.

All the propaganda in the world can't make a cheap suit look good.

Perhaps you were lured by a story on value. Or a wily salesman convinced you that a "four season suit" would be as presentable at 40° below as it would at 98% humidity.

Next time, turn a deaf ear to that snappy patter and turn to Hubert W. White instead. Our helpful clothiers can show you a selection of updated traditionals that are designed to reflect your own personal style. Clothing by Oxxford, sportswear from Perry Ellis, and the finest cotton shirts by Ike Behar, to name just a few.

So before you get caught in the cold war with another bad suit, stop by Hubert W. White and let us show you our autumnal collection of tweeds, cords and flannels.

Hubert W. White

FINE APPAREL FOR MEN AND WOMEN
6o Marquette, Minneapolis · First Bank Building, St. Paul

Store: Hubert W. White
Award Category: Silver Second —
                    Stores Under $5
                    million

A humorous approach made this Hubert W. White suit ad catchy and informative. Hubert W. White simply presents their merchandise to the customer.

Store: Hubert W. White
Award Category: Merit — Stores Under $5 million

A humorous magazine-type ad was employed for Hubert W. White's campaign on men's dress shirts. The bold type used captures the reader's attention and reveals the purpose of the ad.

Are you doing nine to five in the same old pinstripe shirt?

A favorite fashion statement, worn once too often, can become a life sentence. But during the month of June, Hubert W. White is offering freedom of choice with the most outstanding presentation of Kenneth Gordon pinpoint oxford shirts the Twin Cities has ever seen.

Crafted from the finest cotton yarns for added sheen and luxury these extraordinary shirts are available in 26 different sizes and button-down, tab, English spread and classic cricket collar styles.

And because variety is, after all, the spice of life, our repertoire of colors include pink, lavender, ecru, blue, white and various snappy stripes.

So why look like a convict when, instead, Hubert W. White can help you dress like a man of conviction.

Hubert W. White
FINE APPAREL FOR MEN AND WOMEN

Store: Raleigh's
Award Category: Second — Silver
Merchandise $50-100
million

Raleigh's playfully uncovers a new trend in men's boxer shorts. Note the quartered pictures, sparse type, and straightforward copy enhance the product's impact.

FEELING ANTSY?

BIG BUCKS!

PIG HEAVEN!

SELLING SHORT!

R A L E I G H S

Store: Carlisle's

Award Category: Merit — $25-50 million

Carlisle's cartoon ad stresses the "dress for success" concept of today's male executive. The bold type along the bottom of the ad clearly states: "where you can afford the best."

Store: Emporium Capwell
Award Category: Merit — Over $250 million

The "couples" ad stresses the many different components that comprise the wardrobes of to-day's fashion-conscious shopper.

COUPLES

Store: Raleigh's
Award Category: First — Gold Campaigns $50-100 million

Classic, elegant tuxedo-dressing is highlighted in these Raleigh's Formalwear ads. The brief ad descriptions and understated company name enhance the elegance of this ad.

THE CASE OF THE MISSING SIZES IS SOLVED: YOU'LL FIND THEM AT NORDSTROM.

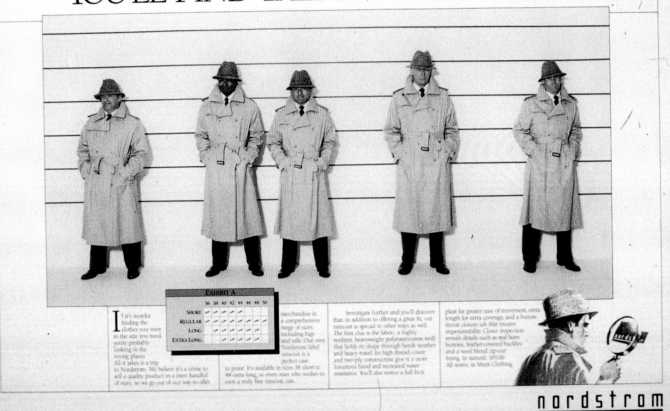

nordstrom

WHEN IT COMES TO PAJAMAS, YOU CAN REST ASSURED WE HAVE YOUR SIZE

nordstrom

Store: Nordstrom's
Award Category: Second — Over $250 million

The difficulty many men face with a proper fit is comically demonstrated in this ad. Nordstrom's boasts that it offers a proper fit to all customers.

Come See Our New Fall Lines.

Join us for our Fall Festival Open House at our new Woodlake Square store, Saturday, September 12.

Our second Houston store at 9696 Westheimer at Gessner is now open. It's filled with our brand new arrivals of classic fall clothing for men and women. And we'd love you to come by and see it all. You'll be suitably impressed.

Refreshments will be served. As will you by our staff of knowledgeable salespeople who are waiting to make you feel as good as they'll make you look.

Come see our new place. Our Open House begins at 10 am. Our commitment to serving you never ends.

9696 Westheimer at Gessner/785-0466
2030 W. Gray Street/523-7077

Jºs.A.Bank
Clothiers

Business has never looked better.

We welcome The American Express® Card, VISA and MasterCard.

Store: Jos. A. Bank Clothiers
Award Category: Merit — Merchandise Ads $100-250 million

To promote their annual fall sale, Jos. A. Bank's chose a novel approach — a colorful autumn leaf that doubles as a pocket handkerchief. The fall sale theme is presented and attention is drawn to the stylized sketch of the suit.

Store: N.B.O.

Award Category: First — $25-50 million

These description filled illustrative ads inform potential customers of the values and quality available at N.B.O. A bright red was used as a second color to emphasize their slogan "everything except shoes."

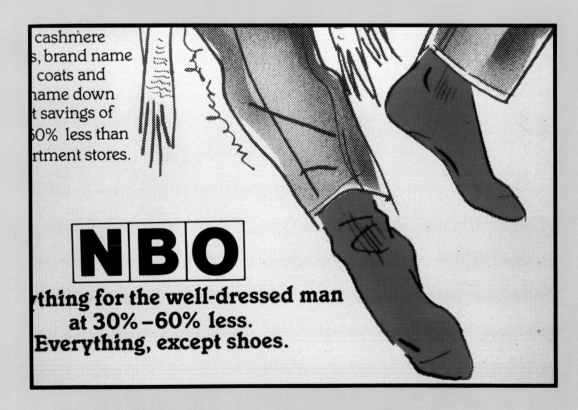

Full Battle Gear For All The Power Plays, Politicking And Hostile Takeovers.

Doing business can be serious business. It has its own set of unique rules, strategies and maneuvers. And, of course, its own uniform.

We're J'S A. Bank and for over 75 years we've defined the look that means business. Classic clothing for men and women in traditional styles that never go out of style.

Our fine garments are made by our own meticulous craftsmen, allowing us to control both quality and costs. Which enables us to price our clothing at an incomparable value.

As for service, our expert salespeople know our business as well as you know yours.

Come to J'S A. Bank. We'll make sure you look good. Even if things get ugly.

Business has never looked better.

J'S.A.Bank Clothiers

Store:	Jos. A. Bank Clothiers
Award Category:	Merit — Merchandise Ads $100-250 million

Professional dressing, fine crafts-manship and knowledgable salespeople are proclaimed in this Jos. A. Bank Clothiers' ad.

Store: Neiman Marcus

Award Category: Merit —
Institutional
Advertisement

Classic two-color illustrations highlight Neiman Marcus' Britain Then
and Now Campaign.

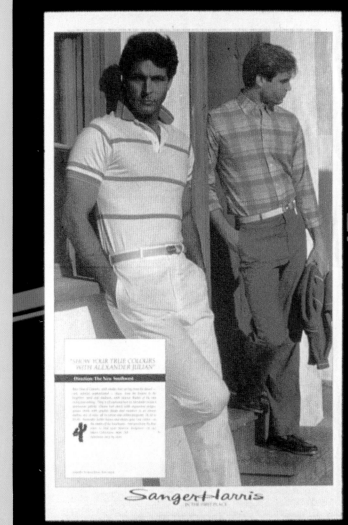

Store: Sanger Harris
Award Category: Merit — Stores over $100 million

This ad displays comfortable casual fashion for summer menswear.

"Dad says I'm the real secret behind his success."

Not that I tell him what to do, because he's a pretty independent guy. But he sees me cracking those books, working so hard, getting ready for some really great school...so he feels he better keep up. And, boy, does he! With plenty of late hours. Weekends, sometimes. Mom and I don't like that too much...but we understand. Anyhow, Dad tells me how proud he is of me. But I'm really proud of him. And I'm going to show him how much I care on Father's Day. He's getting the best present ever, from his favorite store, Saks. And then he can say I'm sure, the secret behind me. Fashion success. I'm that going to far?

The gift of love...the tradition continues.

From Saks's noteworthy collection of sweaters, each one handsomely designed, the textured interest of woven cotton. From Ron Chereskin. Sizes S,M,L,XL, $200. Men's Sweater Collections, Street Floor.

"Dad keeps me ahead of the pack."

And that's pretty tough to do around my neighborhood. The competition's hot. So whenever I feel I'm not on top of things, Dad gets out there and helps. And I end up on top. Because Dad's taught me that you don't give up. How do you think I'm learning to ride this bike? With a lot of scraped knees...and his help! Well, now that it's almost Father's Day, I've got to get him something great. Mom says we'll go to Saks. Dad's got his own special salesperson there who knows just what he likes. And I guess he does, because the way Dad dresses sure keeps him ahead of the pack. Father's Day...the tradition continues.

From Saks's comprehensive Polo collection by Ralph Lauren, the white rugby shirt, sizes S,M,L,XL, $45. The white shorts, 30 to 38, $30. Both in cotton. In the Polo Shop on Six.

"Dad always said I'd end up in braces."

Which sort of confused me, 'cause my teeth are even straighter than his. But, I said, if I could look like him I'd go along with it. Of course, I didn't know he meant suspenders! That just shows you my Dad's sense of humor. Runs in our family. Even Grandad comes up with some funny lines. Guess they take after me. All I know is that I'm really going to surprise Dad this Father's Day. Mom and I are going in on it together. She's pretty sharp...knows just where to go...Saks Fifth Avenue. Nothing ho-hum about the gifts there. They have things my Dad would never even think of. And this year I get to pick him out. Better brace yourself, Dad!

The gift of love...the tradition continues.

From our distinguished and diversified collection of men's braces in cottons and silks. Clockwise from left: "Les Quatre Saisons" pure silk from Trafalgar, $60. Our exclusive cotton madras design, $230. Cotton floral braces, $230. Both, from our Private Label Collection. In Men's Belt Collections, Street Floor.

Store: Saks Fifth Avenue

Award Category: First — Gold Campaigns Over $250 million

The joys of fatherhood and the joy of shopping at a high-quality, traditional, fashionable store are demonstrated in these Saks Fifth Avenue "Father's Day" ads.

Store:	Nordstrom's
Award Category:	Second — Silver
	Inserts Stores Over
	$250 million

Nordstrom's witty camel hair coat ad reinforces a concept Nordstrom is continuously promoting — "Proper fit can be found at Nordstrom's, no matter what size you are."

WHEN IT COMES TO CAMEL'S HAIR SPORT COATS, WE'RE THE LEADERS IN SIZE SELECTION.

"Nice place to discover, but just try to keep warm." So said Jacques Cartier's men when they sailed back from Canada. And the search was on for the perfect outerwear. The voyageurs had the first sensible solution. They observed the native population and adopted the natural skins of the land. But while their coats were warm, they didn't exactly make a fashion statement. Canadians ran through every expedient from the horse blanket to the buffalo coat, before an unnamed genius put together two more natural elements – cotton and down – and created a coat that did it all. It was warm, it was light, it was handsome. Jacques Cartier would have given his eye teeth for one.

Pure cotton down-filled stadium jacket, $325. Harry has down-filled jackets in various lengths and styles, from bomber to stadium jackets, from $245 to $395.

HARRY ROSEN
TORONTO OTTAWA MONTREAL QUEBEC WINNIPEG EDMONTON CALGARY VANCOUVER

WEST EDMONTON MALL 444-1637 • MON.-FRI. 9:30 A.M.-9:00 P.M. SAT. 9:30 A.M.-5:30 P.M. SUN. 12 NOON-5:00 P.M. • EDMONTON CENTRE 425-5373
You can have the Harry Rosen Report on Men's Wear, Fall/Winter '87 edition by sending $5.00 to Harry at: 111 Richmond Street West, Suite 218, Toronto M5H 2G4.

Store: Harry Rosen
Award Category: Merit — Merchandise
$50-100 million

The cotton and down stadium jacket offers a sensible solution in the battle against Canada's Arctic winters.

Store: Waldoff's
Award Category: Merit — Newspaper

▶

Waldoff's chose this photographic ad to display their casual clothing, creating a relaxed, weekend feeling.

"There's a difference between clothes I wear, and clothes I love to wear!"

You know the kind...real style for real life. Lucky for me, Waldoff's always knows just what I'm looking for.

Like the new fall clothes by Claiborne for men. The way I see it, comfort's a pick. But what's more, these are natural basics with style, and price that's surprisingly affordable.

Best of all, everytime I wear them (which is every chance I get) they get even better.

It's good to know these days that there are still things you can likely depend on...well-made clothes, your best friend, and Waldoff's.

WALDOFF'S

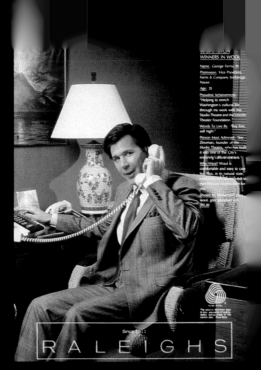

Store: Raleigh's
Award Category: Merit — Campaigns
$50-100 million

Raleigh's interview ads demonstrate two of Washington's great winners — professional achievers and wool suit dressing from Raleigh's.

The New Men's Store at Jordan Marsh... *This is the place!*

Welcome

There's nothing remotely like it anywhere in New England. No where else will you find the selection of quality business clothing, matched with the personal, professional and prompt service your life demands. You need a place that gets down to business and *this is the place!*

Selection

First rate Pure Wool business and casual apparel from such names as Hart, Schaffner & Marx, Mani by Giorgio Armani, JM's own Copley's brand, Austin Reed, Dior Monsieur, Stanley Blacker, Hunter Haig, Milano and Austin Hill. Select from the finest names in professional clothing.

Service

Special service, expressly designed for busy, discriminating, success-oriented men like you. Meet with our personal fashion consultant in the Boston store. Call 357-5597. And rest assured of prompt, knowledgeable shopping assistance from our professional clothing salesmen. They learn your preferences, help you determine what you like in terms of make and style. In short, they sweat the details so you won't have to.

Special

In addition to our full line selections, we've two unique custom programs for men who prefer a more individualized approach to dressing well.
In stock special ordering—preview a specific maker's entire collection, and even though we may not carry your particular size or pattern preference, we will special order at no additional charge. *Custom tailoring*—You'd prefer pleated trousers, no vents, a vest. We can accommodate... for Hart, Schaffner & Marx, we offer the custom fitted program which allows you to virtually design your own suit. Charges commensurate with specific alterations.
And remember, alterations are handled swiftly by our staff of expert tailors.

Convenient

Visit the JM ...red clothing department at ...store most convenient to... ...assachusetts Boston, Framin... ...a, Peabody, Braintree, Burli... ...Worcester Methuen, ...ass. New Hampshire Be... ...mis, New Maine So Port ...Newington Warwick, Conc... ...Rhode Island New York Alb... ...at Waterford

The new-in Woolmark Label is your assurance of quality-tested fabrics made of the world's finest Pure Wool.

Jordan Marsh welcomes the American Express® Card. It's the easy, pleasurable way to discover the most comprehensive selection of menswear in N.E.

Visit the new, totally renovated men's floor on three at JM Boston. More ideas in menswear than you'll find anywhere else.

jordan marsh

children's

In today's society, children's wear is a combination of function and fashion. Children's clothing must be durable enough to last through classrooms and playgrounds, but stylish enough to suit the demands of today's discriminating child.

Children's wear advertising must appeal to adults as that "innocence of childhood," while showing durability and value. Children must approve of the actual merchandise, since they are the real-life models.

Children's ads must appeal to the consumer and entice them to buy fashionable clothing and accessories for their children as well as themselves.

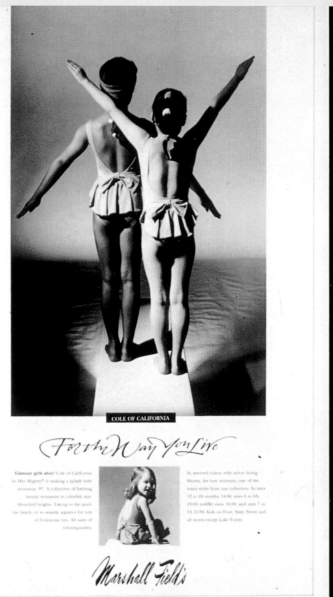

Store: Marshall Fields
Award Category: First — Gold Campaign
Over $250 million

Marshall Fields utilized these "glamour-girls" in Cole of California swimwear to represent their children's swimwear line.

Store: Ron Jon Surf Shop
Award Category: Second — Silver ROP
◄ Color $5-25 million

A newsletter complete with community service information and available merchandise at the Ron Jon Surf Shop provides shoppers with sales information while providing entertainment.

Store: Woodward's
Award Category: Merit — Stores over $100 million

Woodward's magazine approach to these ads is extremely effective through the use of large four-color photographs dealing with a single subject. Notice large display type evokes an emotional response to the picture appearing in that particular ad.

Store: The Boston Store
Award Category: Second — Silver ROP
Color Over $250 million

Crayoned headlines, discounted prices and top name manufacturers highlight these Boston Store kids ads.

Store: Trimingham
              Brothers
Award Category: First — $5-25
              million

This "puppy love" advertisement
lets the customer know that
Trimingham's can supply man
with his "best friend."

Store: Saks Fifth Avenue
Award Category: Second Prize —
              Over $250 million ➤

Saks Fifth Avenue demonstrates the
reinstitution of tradition and charm
in this ad for children's wear. The
tartan pattern and beret evoke time-
less style.

Puppy Love

Tartan:

A Tradition

Charmed!

An enduring delight.

That triumphant pattern

of color/pattern play.

Clan-proud.

All-adored.

Now, sweetened?

Lightened

with eyelet, bows.

A splendid tradition

begun once again

at Saks Fifth Avenue.

Florence Eisman.

Saks Fifth Avenue

The lightweight tartan in green/navy cotton for sizes 4 to 6X, $64. Also, for toddlers, $58. In the Florence Eisman Shop in K.I.D.S. on 8. Tomorrow, from 10 to 6, come meet our special Florence Eisman representative, Ellen Schotte, and see the vast Eisman collection for back-to-school and the holidays. Enjoy a special fashion show at 2 p.m.

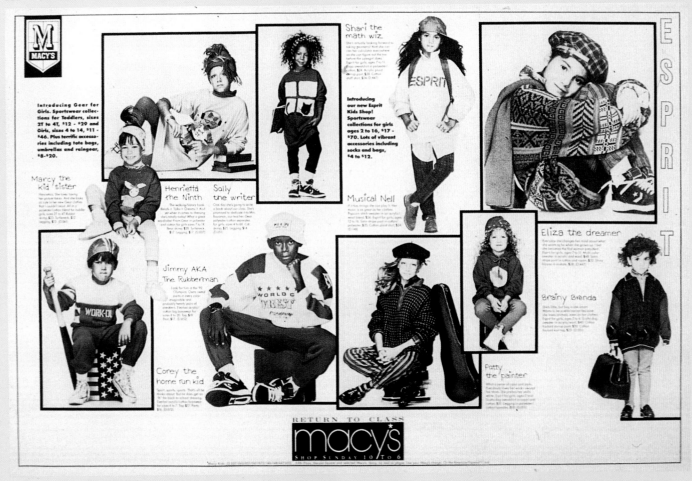

Eliza the dreamer

Everyday she changes her mind about what she wants to be when she grows up. I bet she becomes the first woman president. Esprit for girls, ages 7 to 11. Multi-color sweater in acrylic and wool, $48. Satin stripe pant in cotton and rayon, $32. Shiny blouse in acetate, $28. (D.447)

Sally the writer

One day she's going to write a book about our class. She's promised to dedicate it to Mrs. Bausman, our teacher. Gear polyester/cotton separates for girls, sizes 4 to 6X. Cat skimp, $25. Legging, $14.

Macy's children wear ad evokes the potential of these soon-to-be adults. Several careers and professions are playfully illustrated alongside Gear-wear for kids.

Store: Haughland's Kids
Award Category: First — Gold
Campaigns $5-25
million

Interviews and stylish sportswear
are cleverly combined in these
Haughland's Kids ads.

Store: Marshall Fields
Award Category: Merit — Campaign
Over $250 million

Muffling's sportswear for little girls
is sweetly displayed in this "For
the Way You Live" campaign for
Marshall Fields.

...cleverly offers a great opportunity to start a wardrobe for a new infant or toddler, at discounted prices. The usual clichés have been avoided and the newer trends in design utilized. (Note the large, centrally displayed photograph).

"WE'VE GOT THE CUTEST LITTLE BABY SALE!"

There's not another one could take its place baby sale! Each of our stores will be jumping... this could be the start of something—a great new wardrobe for your infant or toddler. Here's just a tiny sample of clothing and accessories now at big savings.

Marshall Field's

For The Way You Live

Store: ZCMI
Award Category: First — $100-250 ◄ million

Children's wear that is playful yet stylish is pronounced in this ad for ZCMI.

KID TALK.

Amy O'Connor, Age 11

LAST BOOK READ:
Instruction manual for a Macintosh.

FAVORITE QUOTE:
"This year's team captain is Amy O'Connor."

GOALS:
To race on the Olympic ski team.

MAJOR ACCOMPLISHMENT:
Surviving her first dance recital at the Ordway.

PHILOSOPHY:
Kids can do anything they put their minds to.

FAVORITE STORE:
Haugland's Kids

Announcing a kids' clothing store like you've never seen before. Two powerful names have joined to become one. Bringing you the unique selection of first quality name brand and designer clothing you've always found at Haugland's—combined with the value pricing of Kidsmart. Together, we're now 11 "superstores." Where you can count on truly outstanding savings on the brands and styles you're looking for, day in and day out.

Below-retail prices—every day, every item—on top quality, name brand kids' clothes for infants through boys and girls size 14.

HAUGLAND'S KIDS

Store: Haughland Kids
Award Category: Second — Institutional

Haughland's Kids featured these photographic interview ads to demonstrate the practicality and style of their children's clothing.

KID TALK.

Shannon, Age 4.

LAST BOOK READ:
"A Cat in the Hat." Seuss is the only doctor that makes her giggle.

MAJOR ACCOMPLISHMENT:
Learning to ride a two wheel bike (with training wheels), and only scraping one knee.

GOAL:
To have an office just like Mommy's.

SECRET WISH:
To go to school on the bus with my big sister.

FAVORITE QUOTE:
"Here she comes, Miss America."

FAVORITE FOOD:
Catsup. On everything!

FAVORITE STORE:
Haugland's Kids.

We score A+ for back-to-school shopping.
Shopping Haugland's Kids will save you time, money and a lot of running around. You'll find all the clothes your kids will need to get them (and you) through this school year. We carry only first quality merchandise in favorite name brands. Always at our special everyday savings, comparable to other stores' sale prices. So don't learn the hard way. Stop by and give us a test. We're sure to score straight A's for price, quality, selection and convenience.

Low-low prices—every day—on top quality, name brand kids' clothes for infants through boys and girls size 14.

HAUGLAND'S KIDS

Store: Globman's
Award Category: Merit — Campaigns
                   Stores $5-25 million

Globman's employed St. Nickosaur in an unusual Yuletide setup with prehistoric scenes and a "Step-In-Time" visual display traveling exhibit from the Virginia Museum of Natural History. For each dinosaur sold, Globman's contributed $1.00 to the museum. The ads stirred interest and created consumer awareness to this witty marketing technique.

Chapter Four

accessories

Accessories must complement an ensemble without overpowering the entire look. In today's fashion world, accessories must be interesting, tasteful and unique. Jewelry, handbags, neckties, belts and sunglasses all carry a large variety of designer labels offering a range of choices and styles.

More freedom and greater availability must be employed in today's advertising. Trends must be demonstrated alongside traditional classic looks, while maintaining a standard of good taste. Today's working people cannot run from shop to shop or boutique to boutique to find just the right finishing touch to every outfit. Formalwear accessories must be available alongside activewear to allow today's consumer one stop accessorizing. The advertising of fashion accessories must entice the recipient while endorsing style, fashionability and quality.

Store: SM Shoemart
Award Category: Merit — $25-50
million

This SM Shoemart ad uses a gangster theme to promote an air of mystery and intrigue. The large black and white photograph and the sparseness of type makes this ad appear as if it was printed in the earlier part of the 20th century.

Store: Mayor's Jewelers
Award Category: Second — $25-50 million

This ad shows that jewelry is not only fashionable, but a great gift idea. The simple businesslike attire of the model offsets the sparkling glamour of gold.

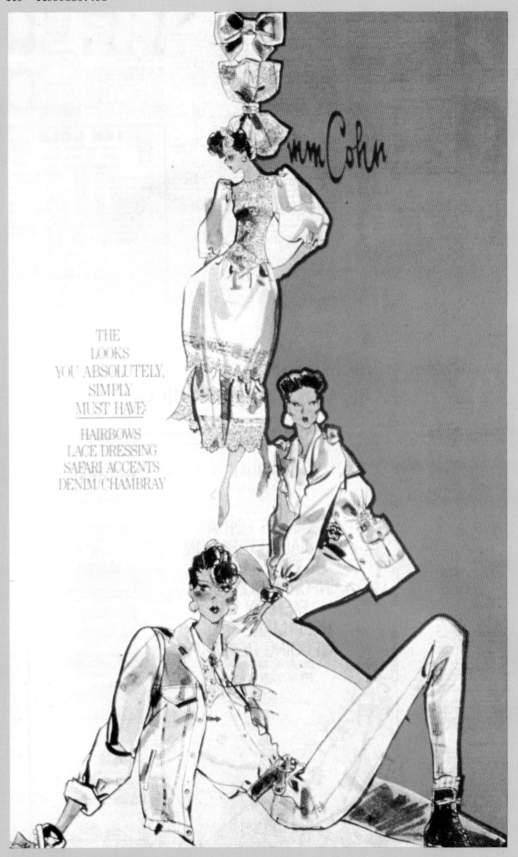

Store: M.M. Cohn
Award Category: Merit — Merchandise
                    $25-50 million

Fashion sketches and a brief accessory list alert the customer to what's available at M.M. Cohn's, in a concise, direct manner.

What's better than a grand opening sale?

Some shoe stores have a grand opening sale where they feature a few brand names. So you go to the store and find out those brand names aren't in style or they're "seconds", or sometimes even both.

At Brandstand, brand name shoes are all we feature. All in the latest women's, men's, and athletic styles. All first quality. And all 20 to 50% less than retail. Names like 9 West, Bass, Adidas, Bally, Mushrooms, Etienne Aigner,

Clark's of England, Johnston & Murphy, Streetcars, Miramonte, Nina, Hipoppotamus, Jarman, Wm Joyce, Etonic, Puma, Hang Ten, Rossi, Nettleton, Gloria Vanderbilt, Updates, Naturalizer, Surfriders, Bill Blass; you get the idea. And now, during our brand opening sale, you can save an extra $5.00 with the coupon below on any pair of shoes at Brandstand.

A brand opening coupon.

Store: Brandstand
Award Category: Merit — Stores
Under $5 million

A direct marketing approach is used in this advertisement. A discount coupon, bold typeface, and well-known quality brandnames create a potential customer loyalty to Brandstand's shoes in this black and white ad.

Retail Price $34.00
Brandstand Price
$16.

Retail Price $35.00
Brandstand Price
$19.

Retail Price $50.00
Brandstand Price
$30.

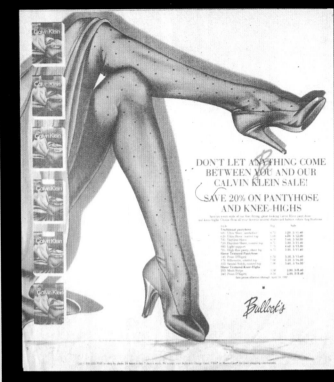

Store: Bullock's
Award Category: Award of Merit/
                    Merchandise/Over $250
                    million

Bullock's employed this fashionable
illustration to demonstrate their
"Traditions" apparel campaign.

Store: Dayton's
Award Category: Merit — Merchandise
$100-250 million

A teasing headline and a large photographic display of a female tennis player making a serve, promotes the diamond tennis bracelet available at Dayton's.

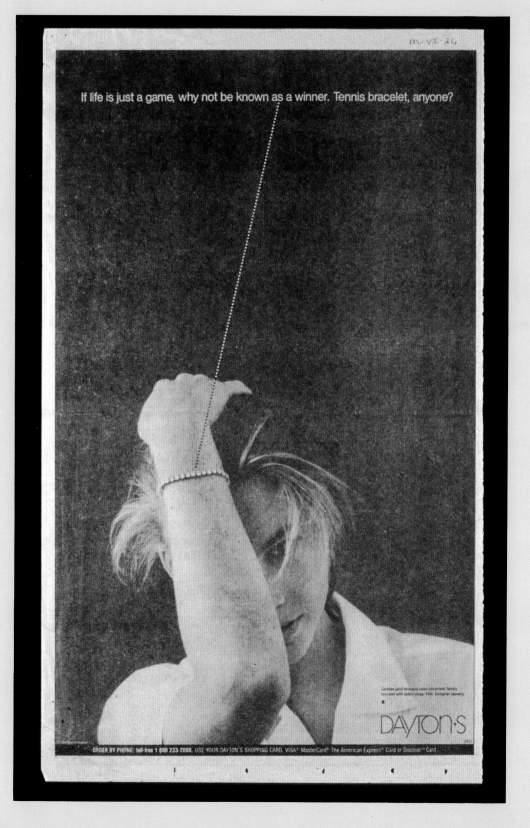

If you love this ad, you must have holes in your head.

Zell Bros has hundreds of ways to fill those tiny holes. At hundreds of different prices, from $20 to $25,000. Now, if you don't happen to have holes in your head, don't despair. We also have a rather impressive collection of clasp-type earrings.

Store: Zell Brothers
Award Category: First — Gold
                    Merchandise $5-25
                    million

Gold, silver, pearls and semi-pre-
cious stones are displayed in this
enticing ad for Zell Brothers
Jewelers. The satirical headline en-
hances the broad appeal of this ad.

Store: Bockstruck's
Award Category: First — Gold
Campaigns Stores
Under $5 million

Bockstruck's utilized witty phrases and clear photographs to promote their jewelry fashion shows.

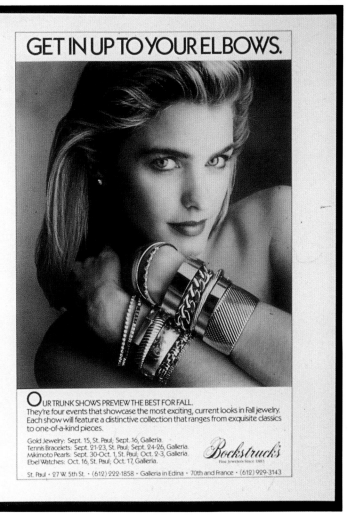

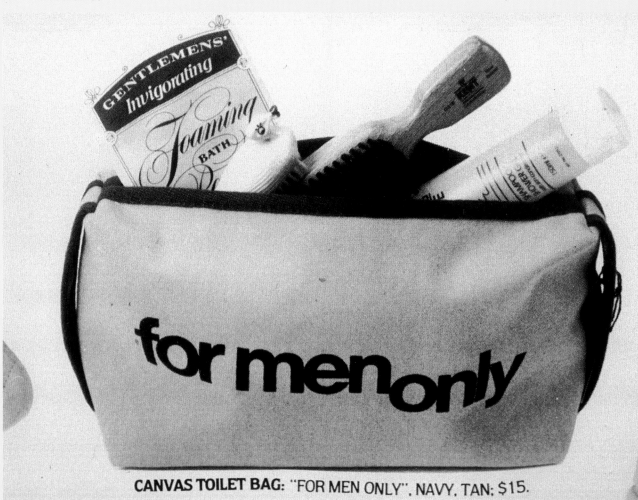

CANVAS TOILET BAG: "FOR MEN ONLY", NAVY, TAN: $15.

H: GREEN. $3.50.

RED, YELLOW, BLUE: $1.40.

SH:

MINI DART SET

MINI DART SET: BOARD AND DARTS IN CASE: $13.

Store: H.A. & E. Smith Ltd.
Award Category: First — $5-25 million

Unique gift ideas accentuate this Father's Day ad. Copy information about the products was wrapped around each photograph for a stronger visual impact in overall layout.

Store: Bullock's
Award Category: Merit — Over $250 million

Bullock's dazzling jewelry availability is reinforced by this sparkling illustration that hints at regality.

Store: Raleigh's
Award Category: First — Gold Campaign
$50-100 million

The elegance and fine art of footwear are displayed in this Salvatore Ferragamo ad for Raleigh's that appeared in the magazine section of the Washington Post's "Tribute to Elegance" in September, 1987.

american fragrance

America's own designers have a tremendous influence on how the whole world looks, lives, even smells. Here, our own favorite fragrances from the collections on our main floor (Fifth Avenue) and all our branches. And during the next two weeks, when you purchase 25.00 or more of any of these scents, you'll receive a tote-ful of sample size scents at no extra cost.

Store: Maison Blanche
Award Category: Merit — Newspaper

Magie Noire perfume by Lancome is highlighted in this mysterious photographic ad. Maison Blanche uses French undertones to the classic American Christmas theme.

Store: B. Altman's
Award Category: First — $100-250 million
◄

Altman's patriotism is exemplified in this American salute to designer fragrances for both men and women.

Midwest Vision Center's chic portrait of this model with sunglasses and black lace head scarf evoke an appeal to glamour-conscious eyeglass wearers.

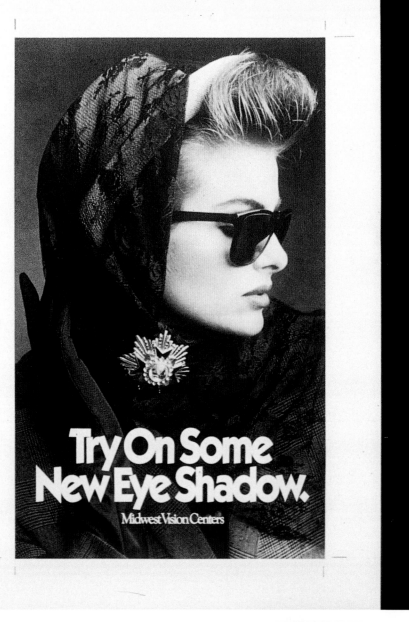

Store: Midwest Vision
Award Category: Second — Stores
                    $5-25 million

Extremely bold type and product offering enhance this direct approach ad.

Male vanity is satirically ruffled with this portrait ad.

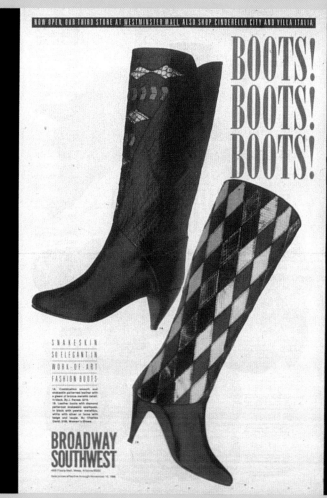

Store: Broadway

Award Category: Merit — Newspaper Inserts

Western boots in nontraditional colors, leathers, and suedes highlight this ad.

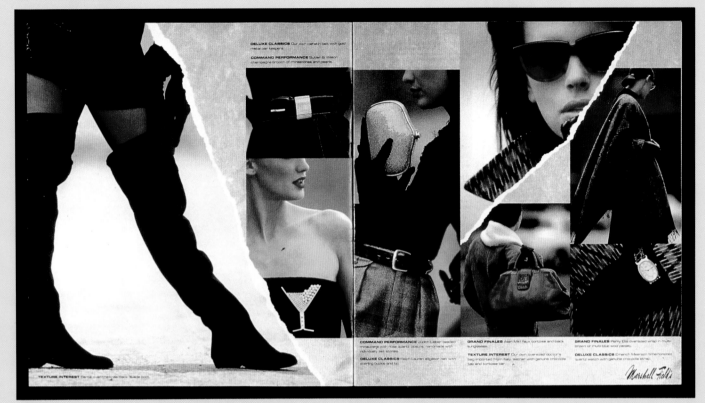

Store: Marshall Fields
Award Category: First — Gold
              Merchandise Ads Over
              $250 million

Marshall Fields displays an array of
sharp accessories in this collage-
type ad offering everything from
belts to evening bags for the fash-
ion-minded shopper.

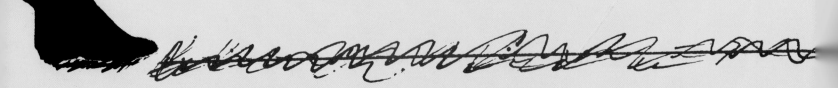

Store: Bullock's

Award Category: Merit — Over $250 million

Bullock's use of black and white reinforces the "1940s glamour appeal" of these ads for high-heeled shoes, silky blouses for larger women, and Givenchy patterned pantyhose. The chorus girl layout of the Givenchy advertisement is reminiscent of the style of a bygone era.

Store: Dayton's
Award Category: Merit — Merchandise
◄ Ads Over $250 million

Dayton's employed a collage type ad
to demonstrate the availability of
shoes for "all walks of life from tod-
dlers to adults."

Store: Brown's Shoe Stop
Award Category: Merit — $25-50
million

Brown's fashion illustrative ad represents shoes that include a retro
lizard skin wingtip and glitzy contemporary pump for today's fashionable woman. The oversized picture
adds tremendous graphic impact for
an up-to-date look.

Nordstrom's proudly salutes traditional American footwear with these saddleshoe and boat shoe ads.

These fashion sketched ads accentuate Nordstrom's "first class" approach to contemporary fashion. The black and white drawings perform equally well for many forms of apparel. Elegance is emphasized through the use of contrasting black and white.

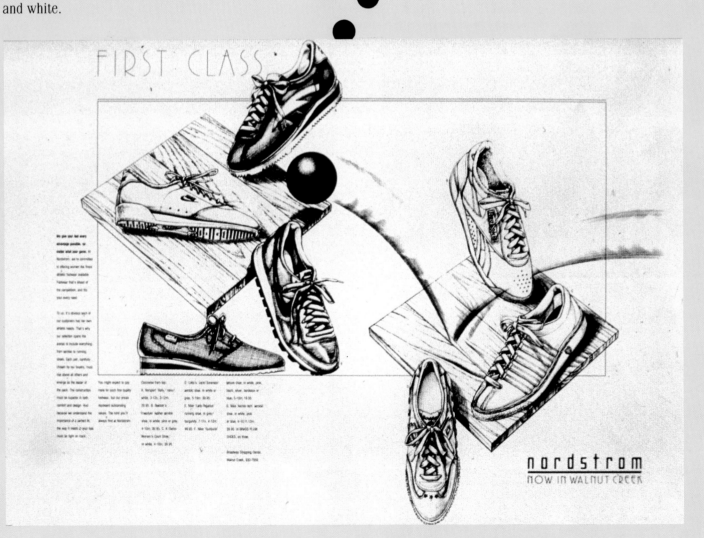

Store: Hofheimer's
Award Category: Merit — Campaigns
$5-25 million

These Hofheimer shoe ads offer fashionable footwear for your first few steps or your millionth and first step, at affordable prices.

PART II
HOME FASHIONS

Brandstand

Creeds

Midwest Vision Centers

Rich's Elder-Beerman

Waldoff's

IKEA

Winners Apparel, Ltd.

Magasin du Nord

Hubert W. White

Holt Renfrew & Co., Ltd.

Allen Furniture

Glik's Creeds

Hubert W. White The Chesterfield Shop Ltd.

Mayor's Jewelers

ZCMI

H.A. & E. Smith

Crowley's

Haugland's Kids

John Wanamaker

Sanger Harris

Waldoff's Valley View Mall

Godchaux/Maison Blanche Jordan Marsh

Neiman Marcus

Kitchen Bazaar

SM-Shoemart

Donaldsons

McCurdy's

Cohoes
Specialty Stores

Adam, Meldrum
& Anderson

Stewart's

B. Altman
The Broadway
Marshall Field
& Co.

Carson Pirie Scott

Racquet Sports
Group of Canada

Lipton's
Heritage House

Macy's

Bath 'N Bedtime

Dayton Hudson
Nordstrom
Raleighs

Gantos

Thalhimers

Macy's
Bullock's
Thalhimers

NBO Stores, Inc.

Neiman-Marcus
Nordstrom

Today, furniture advertising is a multifaceted field. While many varieties are offered, the ads must allow the customer to maintain one's own personal tastes in choosing fabrics, styles and colors. Traditional, country, hi-tech, and contemporary furniture must be readily available to the consumer.

Many homes today employ a blending of these styles, not merely one theme or concept. An individual home decorator may choose to follow one particular theme down to the tiniest detail. Often, furniture ads must persuade the customer and offer assurance and acceptability toward the concept of removing all existing furniture and starting over again for a fresh, new look. Furniture ads enforce the concept that our surroundings do directly influence our personalities and the way other people perceive us.

Cross someone off your Christmas list.

With a unique gift idea to warm a home. Or trim a tree. Including candlesticks, pillows, brass items, mugs, dishes, placemats, vases, Christmas tree skirts and ornaments. At prices that will please a generous Santa. Or a tightfisted Scrooge. Like our $1500 adult-sized rocking horse. Or a rocking horse ornament for just a dollar. Spread at least $10 of holiday cheer and the gift-wrapping is free. Drop by Chanhassen. When you want to drop some names from your list.
Next to the Dinner Theatres, Chanhassen, MN.
Tuesday through Saturday 9-9, Monday 9-5. 612/934-1521

CHANHASSEN
FURNITURE GALLERIES

Our sale prices on upholstered furniture won't cost you an

and a

If you've always wanted a traditional, quality sofa or chair from Chanhassen, now's the time to buy. Our upholstered furniture is 20% to 50% off. Special orders are available too. Choose your style. Choose your fabric. But choose soon. This sale ends August 31. So shake a leg.
Next to the Dinner Theatres, Chanhassen, MN.
Tuesday through Saturday 9-9, Monday 9-5. 612/934-1521

CHANHASSEN
FURNITURE GALLERIES

Store: Chanhassen Furniture
Award Category: Gold First — Stores Under $5 million

Chanhassen Furniture used a unique satirical approach to their furniture sales. The arm and leg ad employs an old cliche to appeal to the budget-minded consumer. The Christmas List ad reminds the customer about Chanhassen's gifts and accessories for the home. The Musical Chairs ad informs the customer that if Chanhassen's runs out of stock on a particular item they will "special order it for you."

Store: ZCMI
Award Category: Second — $100-250
                    million

This colorful collage displaying
housewares, home furnishings, and
electronic equipment epitomizes
ZCMI's appeal to the metropolitan
consumer.

Store: Century Furnishings
Award Category: Merit — ROP Color
Under $5 million

Bright, colorful leather sofas and marble end tables represent affordable home-decorating from Century Furnishings. These colored bordered ads coordinate with the colors of the displayed merchandise.

Store: Abraham and
                     Strauss
Award Category: Second prize —
                    Over $250 million

This neo-classic black and lacquer
sleep sculpture highlighted
Abraham and Strauss' light and airy
advertisement: The bed's lines follow a traditional four-poster design
— but appear up-to-date in a glossy
black finish.

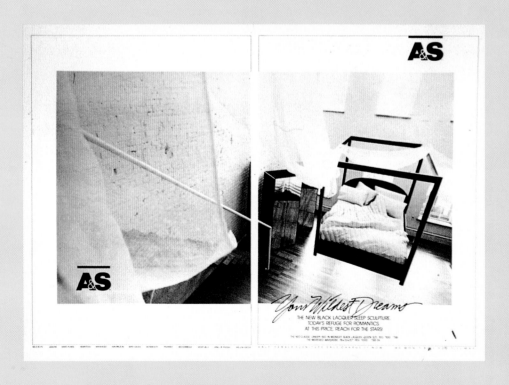

Buy an IKEA bed
and get $50 off the cover price.

BUY ANY BED BEFORE OCT. 31ST AND SAVE $50 ON IKEA BEDDING.

$281

$378

$473

$134

$526

$588

IKEA 1988

For a closer look under the covers of our beds see pages 74–91 of the IKEA catalogue.

$281

IKEA

Swedish for Common Sense.

#2556 – 8770 – 170th Street, West Edmonton Mall. Phone: 444-2345. STORE HOURS: Mon. – Fri. 10 – 9, Sat. 10 – 6, Sun. Noon – 5.

Store: IKEA

Award Category: Second — Silver Sale Ads

IKEA's bed advertisement offers a discount on the large selection of mattresses available from the store that's Swedish for "common sense."

Store: Chesterfield Shop

Award Category: Second — Stores under $5 million

The Chesterfield Shop employed this direct approach to inform their potential customers of the functions, quality, and price of this leather sleep sofa.

Chesterfield's modular grouping ad stresses the economic availability of their home decorating.

IKEA's bookcase ad humorously presents the advantages of shopping at IKEA. Quality, price, and convenience add up to big savings.

Allen Furniture used this ad to inform its potential customers of their winter sale. The penguin implies a formal, yet playful approach to home decorating and reinforces the winter sale theme.

You've seen houses that look like this from the front.
This is how the other half lives.

Store: Fortunoff's
Award Category: Merit — Over $250
                    million

Fortunoff's demonstrates their belief
that a home's outdoor furniture
should be as exquisite as its indoor
furnishings.

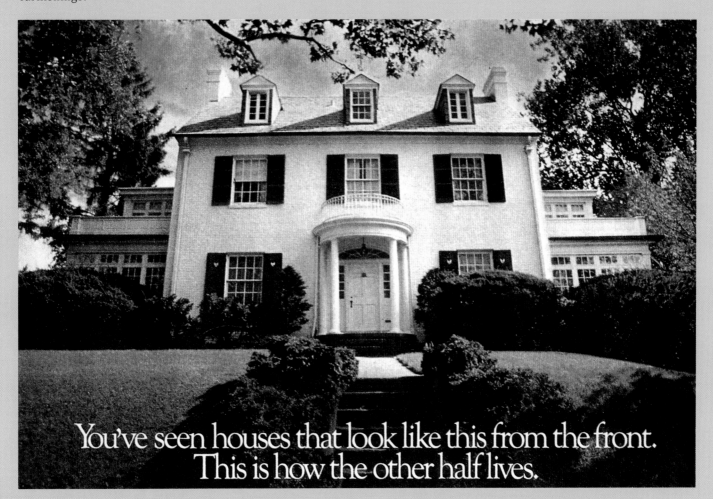

You've seen houses that look like this from the front.
This is how the other half lives.

Chapter Six
housewares

Kitchens are no longer the private dwellings of the homemaker, where an entire day was spent in the preparation of one specific meal. Housewares reflect these changes. Today, many household tasks are divided among family members; therefore, housewares must be practical, efficient, fast and fun. The advertising of these appliances must be attractive to many different types of people.

The influx of healthy eating through healthy food preparation must be presented to the consumer and the newest innovations in food preparation and servewear must be presented. In today's kitchens, housewares must be esthetically pleasing while coordinating with a large variety of styles. The cookware and appliances of the great chefs must be available to the public and these ads must list benefits, extol quality and provide time-saving information in one presentation.

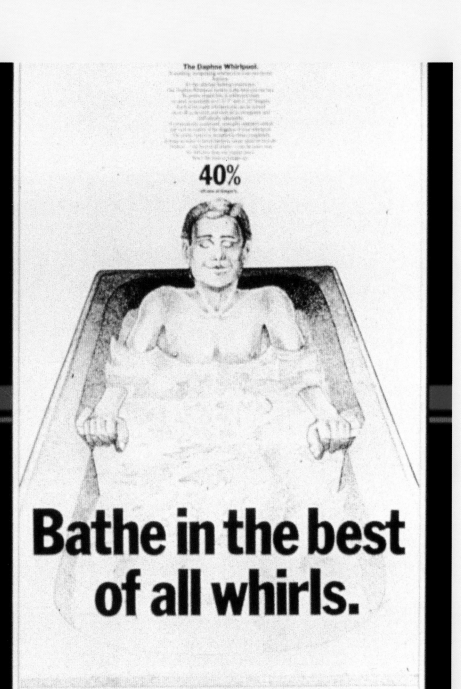

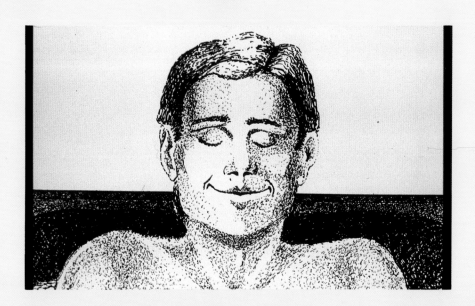

"At
Bath n' Bedtime,
everything
but the
merchandise
is irregular."
You'll see the best first-quality percale sheets, towels and accessories at Bath n' Bedtime.
In a selection that is unbelievably large. It's the biggest choice in Canada. You'll see all the up-to-the-minute looks, from designers and manufacturers you know.
Even our everyday prices are irregular. They're significantly lower than at department and specialty stores.
We guarantee it!
Buying sheets and towels retail and saving at Bath n' Bedtime is becoming the regular thing to do.
Bath n' Bedtime
Where the white sale never ends.
OUR GUARANTEE: We will pay you double the difference if within 15 days of your purchase you can buy the same article for less elsewhere in Canada.

Store: Bath and Bedtime
Award Category: Merit — Stores
under $5 million

Bath and Bedtime offers first-rate, quality merchandise at low prices with these direct approach advertisements. A humorous angle was utilized to breakaway from traditional sales methods for bathroom fixtures.

Store: Trimingham Brothers

Award Category: First — $5-25 million

This interesting ad represented Trimingham's unique approach to display fine crystal stemware. Note the black lacquered hand gives the ad an air of sophistication, yet does so in a playful and modern way.

Store: Emporium Capwell
Award Category: First — Gold Inserts Stores Over $250 million

Emporium Capwell satisfies the customer's need for a store that responds to ideas. This "Home Ideas" ad allows the customer to associate Emporium Capwell with their own home decorating concepts.

HOME IDEAS

New Dansk Mesa china, plus savings for your kitchen, bedroom and more, starting Sept. 25.

EMPORIUM·CAPWELL
has the right idea

Store: Kitchen Bazaar

Award Category: Merit — Stores
Under $5 million

Kitchen Bazaar used these striking white type, white framed ads to create a bold appeal for their discounted housewares.

Store: B. Altman's
Award Category: First — $100-250
                    million

Home furnishings and housewares appear at home in
Altman's country settings and
down home displays.

FREE Six-Pak of Lite!*

No I.D. Required!

Lamps Plus will quench your thirst for the absolute largest selections of both *imported* and *domestic* lamps and lighting fixtures around.

And we'll pour out real and true values and savings on styles to fit just about every taste and decor. And budget too!

Just present this ad with your purchase of *$10 or more*, and we'll give you six-60w Abco™ household bulbs absolutely *FREE!*

And that's a $9.00 value!

Lamps Plus. The absolute largest selections and the greatest values on all types of lighting around. Anywhere.

LAMPS PLUS

GLENDALE
200 S. Brand
(818) 247-3005

Store: Lamps Plus
Award Category: First — Gold
Merchandise Ads Stores
$25-50 million

This ad was aimed at building awareness of their new stores. The offering of a free gift with any purchase catches the consumer's attention in a fun and straightforward manner.

Store: Dayton's
Award Category: Merit — Merchandise
Over $250 million

Dayton's clearly states the uses of their large selection of video and electronic equipment in these bold typefaced ads.

Store: Leggett's
Award Category: Merit — Best Institutional Newspaper

David Hechter's dinnerware, organically-grown juniors wear, and Villeroy and Boch china are all displayed in these STAR-tling merchandise ads for Leggett's.

RETAIL SALES

Curtain Country

At Curtain Country we'd like to offer you something more than just a job.

We'd like to offer you a future where you can go as far as your drive, determination and ambition will take you.

We're not so big that we're impersonal. We're not so small that opportunity is limited by size. We're a fast growing retail firm that treats our employees like family. We extend them the same courtesy and consideration we show our customers, and maybe that's one of the reasons we're growing so fast.

If you come to work for Curtain Country, here's what you'll get -

- *Paid Holidays*
- *Paid Sick Days*
- *Rapidly Accumulated Paid Vacation*
- *Employee Discount Privileges*
- *Disability Pay*
- *Payroll Savings Plan*
- *Promotion and Career Path*

And you'll also find an awfully nice place to work. Come in and see us at a Curtain Country near you - Monday to Saturday, 10 AM to 6 PM; or call our personnel director, Ms. Diamond at 516-483-6272.

- *Valley Stream* • *Carle Place* • *Levittown* • *Huntington*
- *Centereach* • *Lindenhurst* • *Bay Shore* • *Riverhead*

Store: Curtain Country
Award Category: Merit — Best Institutional Newspaper

Curtain Country's storybook ad describes its merchandise and service available in a clear, homey manner. Store locations and phone numbers were inconspicuously placed along the ad's bottom edge.

Make Every Room A Pretty Room.

Curtain Country

Lots And Lots Of Curtains And Other Pretty Things. And, Yes, Lots Of Friendly Service, Too.

The Lovely Story Of Curtain Country

Not too long ago, in a land very close to here (probably only a few miles away) a place was created that was filled with many very lovely things. Curtains, drapes, priscillas, towels, bedspreads, comforters, bath accessories and much more. It was filled with so many pretty things for one very simple reason. To enable you to make your home prettier.

And that, in turn, could make your life a little more pleasant.

This wonderful place was also filled with friendly, courteous people whose one and only task was to help make it easier for you to choose the pretty things that will make your home prettier. At prices that are beautiful, too.

This enchanted place is called Curtain Country. There's probably a Curtain Country near you because there are well over twenty Curtain Country stores in this part of the world. There's even a Curtain Country ad in today's newspaper. Come in soon and see all of the lovely things that can make every room in your home more serene and harmonious. If you do, we promise you'll live prettier ever after.

PART III
PROMOTIONAL

Brandstand

Creeds

Midwest Vision Centers

Rich's Elder-Beerman

Waldoff's

IKEA

Winners Apparel, Ltd.

Magasin du Nord

Hubert W. White

Holt Renfrew & Co., Ltd.

Allen Furniture

Glik's Creeds

Hubert W. White The Chesterfield Shop Ltd.

Mayor's Jewelers

ZCMI

H.A. & E. Smith

Crowley's

Haugland's Kids

John Wanamaker

Sanger Harris

Waldoff's Valley View Mall

Godchaux/Maison Blanche Jordan Marsh

Neiman Marcus

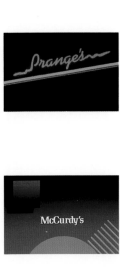

Chapter Seven
store promotions

Store promotion advertising must remind the customer of store policies and services. Luxuries, benefits and special services must be reflected, while stressing the store's appreciation for customer's loyalty. Often, a new theme or benefit is introduced to allow the customer a brief escape from everyday shopping. Positivism must reign over negativism. Shopping in a particular store must be perceived as an adventure, not a chore.

Fashions, glamour, and excitement must be apparent. Store promotion advertising must reassure the consumer that they have made the right decision by shopping at a particular mall, boutique or store.

Store: Neiman Marcus
Award Category: First — Newspaper

Neiman Marcus used this koala bear illustration to assist the launch of the Australian Fortnight campaign.

The dazzling 69-carat black opal, lighting bolt, and black background create a glittering setting for the Australian Fortnight campaign ad.

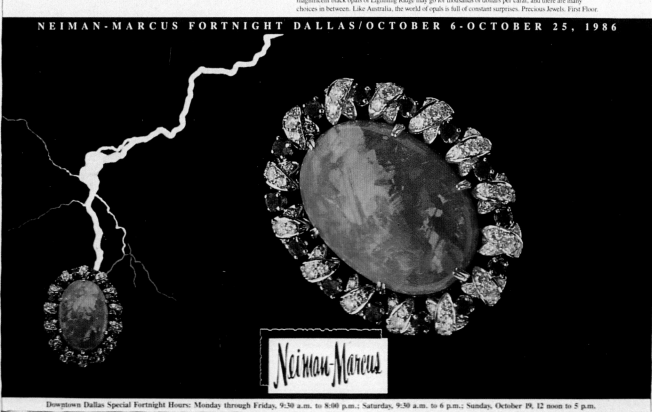

Store: Joseph Spiess

Award Category: Merit — $5-25 million

Joseph Spiess announced the opening of their new Spring Hill branch — under the atrium — with this advertisement.

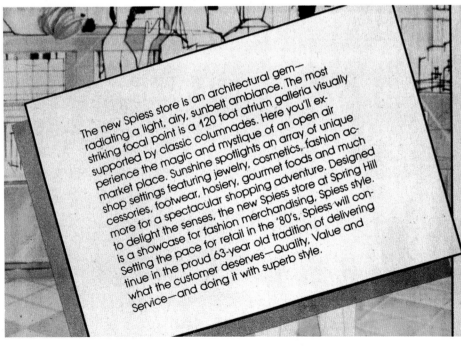

Store: Valley View Mall
Award Category: Merit — Newspaper

Playfull cartoon characters and famous name stores enhance this ad for Valley View Mall. Colorful illustrations highlight this ad announcing the sidewalk sale at Valley View Mall.

Store: Boston University Bookstore

Award Category: Merit — Institutional Advertisement

A large, four-color photograph of a person handbinding a book represents the bookstore's emphasis on quality. The copy "we select books by the size of their ideas, not their publishers" reinforces the bookstore's academic image.

Some of the World's Greatest Ideas Come from Its Smallest Presses.

The world's most innovative, creative thinkers and writers have long depended on small, private presses to communicate their new ideas to a dedicated few. That's why our Charlesbank Bookshop features a section devoted to small publishing houses, for you, that dedicated few.

The Boston University Bookstore's Charlesbank Bookshop. We select books by the size of their ideas, not their publishers.

BOSTON UNIVERSITY BOOKSTORE
660 BEACON STREET · BOSTON

At Kenmore Square. Hours: Mon.-Sat. 9:30am-7pm, Sun 12-5pm. Major credit cards accepted. Validated parking around the corner.

Book binding implements courtesy of Harcourt Bindery, Inc.

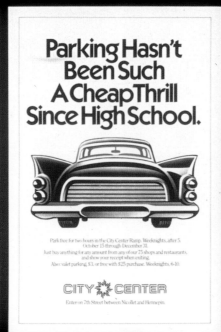

Park Here For Peanuts.

Park free for two hours in the City Center Ramp. Weeknights, after 5. Now through December 31.

Just buy anything for any amount from any of our 75 shops and restaurants, and show your receipt when exiting.

Also: valet parking, $3, or free with $25 purchase. Weeknights, 6-10.

CITY ❈ CENTER

Enter on 7th Street between Nicollet and Hennepin.

Parking Hasn't Been Such A Cheap Thrill Since High School.

Park free for two hours in the City Center Ramp. Weeknights, after 5. October 15 through December 31.

Just buy anything for any amount from any of our 75 shops and restaurants, and show your receipt when exiting.

Also: valet parking, $3, or free with $25 purchase. Weeknights, 6-10.

CITY ❈ CENTER

Enter on 7th Street between Nicollet and Hennepin.

Introducing Our New Customer Service Department.

VALET

Valet parking for $3, or free with $25 purchase, at City Center. Weeknights, 6-10. Now through December 31.

Come enjoy our 75 shops and restaurants while we wait on you from curb to counter.

Also: free parking weeknights, after 5, with any purchase from City Center.

CITY ❈ CENTER

Drop-off at 7th Street Mall entrance, next to the Marriott.

Store: City Center Mall
Award Category: Merit — Shopping Center

These three "parking" ads humorously endorse the availability of parking at City Center Mall.

"Our job at Waldoff's is to make sure you come back."

We are at your service. And so far as we know, there's no one in any store that will help you like we can.

You see, even though Waldoff's hired us, we work for you. And our job is to do just one thing: make you happy.

That goes for anything, anywhere in the store. If you need help, we'll take you step by step. You'll never be abandoned just because we don't normally work in a particular department, or because it may be time for our break.

Suppose you need a special gift. We'll not only make suggestions, we'll wrap it

free, and move heaven and earth to get it delivered at the time you want it, If that is your wish.

And at any time, for any reason, you're not completely satisfied with your purchase, we'll return or exchange it with the same courtesy and smiles you received when you bought it.

Rest assured, you'll never have to come looking for us. We'll be there.

Visit us soon. All of us, plus the other 126 professionals at Waldoff's are here to see that you come back often.

WALDOFF'S

Store: Waldoff's
Award Category: Merit — Institutional

Waldoff's photographically displays several members of their staff to reinforce the concept that Waldoff's wants their customers to return — again and again.

Store: Adam, Meldrum &
             Anderson
Award Category: First — Gold ROP Color
             $100-250 million

Jingle Bear is beautifully displayed
in this ad from Adam, Meldrum &
Anderson. The large four-color, full
page format adds tremendous appeal to the product.

21,106 Sweaters.

We know you want selection when you shop. Lots of it.

Choice and more choice.

Now, every shopping centre will tell you they have selection. But we didn't want to just say it. We wanted to prove it. Dramatically.

So we went round to every clothing merchant in St. Laurent and counted sweaters. Infant sweaters. Young ladies'. Boys'. Women's. Men's sweaters. Everybody's sweaters.

Acrylic. Cotton. Angora. Silk. Every fibre known. Sweaters.

21,106 of them.

That's a lot of counting. But the point is: that's a lot of sweaters for you to choose from.

And because of the number and astonishing variety of stores at St. Laurent, you'll find wide choices in just about any category you care to name. Kitchen appliances. Tennis racquets. Draperies. Shoes.

Wallpaper. Food products.

The selection's going to become even greater, of course, when we add an exciting new group of stores.

Just as we're going to have more parking for you.

And even more convenient bus service.

And all part of a shopping centre that's always easy and convenient to get around in.

Lots of sweaters.

Lots of all the things you want and need.

And always getting better.

St. Laurent Shopping Centre.
It just keeps on getting better!

Store: St. Laurent

Award Category: Merit — Best Institutional Newspaper

This bold typeface ad "counts" the benefits of shopping at St. Laurent's Shopping Centre. Housewares, sporting goods, food, and clothing are all stressed to reinforce the convenience of mall shopping.

Store: Raleigh's
Award Category: First — Gold Sale Ads

Simplicity, witty copy and unique
graphics create a novel concept to
demonstrate Raleigh's sale.

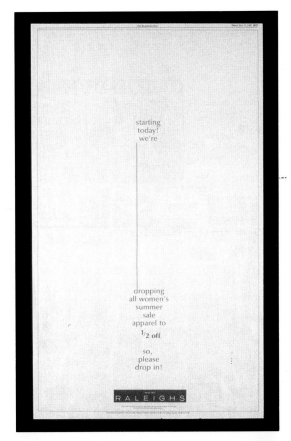

Store: Dayton's
Award Category: First — Gold
                     Institutional

Dayton's announces the return of
Santa Bear in this two-sided ad.
"He's back, but not for long" is
cleverly shown by the front and
back of the bear.

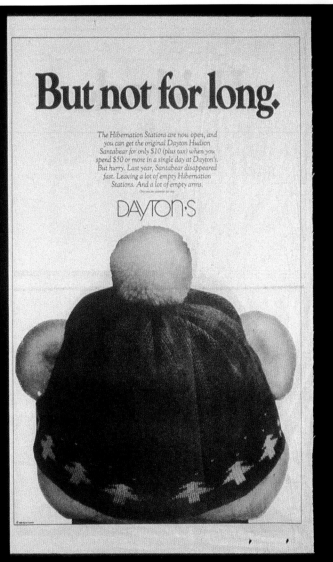

Store: M.M. Cohn
Award Category: Merit — Color $25-50 million

M.M. Cohn directs shoppers to stop tracks and shop at M.M. Cohn in this clever store promotion ad. The advertisement also reminds shoppers to drive carefully.

Store: Bullock's
Award Category: Merit — Merchandise
Over $250 million

Bullock's employed this fashionable
illustration to demonstrate their
"Traditions" apparel campaign.'

Relax.

You've still got 20 days 'til Christmas. So make out your shopping list and spend just one of those days at IKEA.

IKEA is filled with all kinds of things your friends and relatives never knew they always wanted. Functional things that make fun gifts. Unique things that make useful gifts.

On Christmas morning they'll open their gifts and exclaim, "Where did you ever find it?" And you'll just smile and tell them you're glad they like it.

Because, if it's better to give than to receive, then where you spend before Christmas, can be almost as important as where you spend Christmas.

We're Stuffing Stockings.

OK, kids. If you think you've been good this year, bring in your left sock to IKEA before closing time on Sunday, December 8.

Your sock will be magically stuffed with Christmas goodies. (But remember, that's your left sock. And not your Dad's, either!) Then, on Saturday or Sunday, December 14 and 15, you can pick up your seasonally stuffed stocking in the store. If you've been good, that is.

Improve The Food Bank's Balance.

Christmas is a time for sharing and caring.

This year, open your hearts and your cupboards to those who are less fortunate.

Bring your donations of canned and dry goods for the Food Bank to IKEA and we'll match each donation with a donation of our own.

Give Us Your Kids For Christmas.

Christmas may be for kids, but Christmas shopping is for parents.

So, while you're shopping at IKEA, we'll mind the kids in our Ballroom (3 to 7 years old, please).

But, rest assured, no matter how much you protest, we'll give them back when you want to leave.

Many Happy Returns.

Some people are never satisfied.

So, in the unlikely event that any of your friends or relatives wish to return or exchange their IKEA gifts, we'll be happy to oblige. After all, how were you to know Aunt Gwen already had a turquoise leather Goteborg sofa?

To avoid any misgivings, any IKEA gift purchased between November 15/85 and December 24/85 may be returned for a full refund or exchange until January 12, '86. For complete details on our return policy, see page 7 of the yellow pages in our 1986 catalogue. Items may be returned to any IKEA in Canada with proof of purchase.

IKEA

Christmas well spent.

Store: Ikea

Award Category: Second — $100-250 million

The powerful use of white in coordination with columnar type creates a unique, out-of-the-ordinary Christmas advertisement.

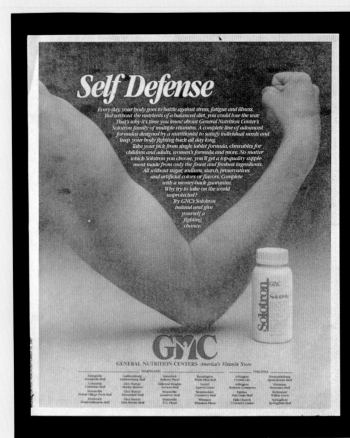

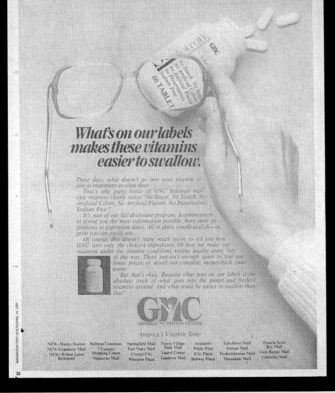

Store: General Nutrition Center

Award Category: Merit — Campaigns Over $250 million

General Nutrition Center employs ads that promote the benefits of their vitamins and products. The benefit is the lack of additives and other un-natural ingredients.

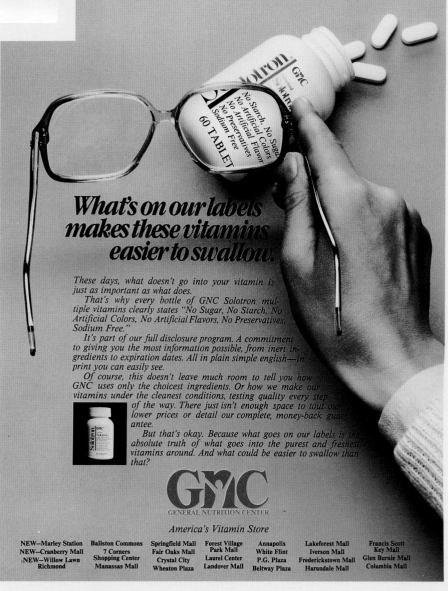

Store: Prange's
Award Category: Merit — Best Institutional Newspaper

Prange's employed a simplistic approach in this cartoon ad announcing their new store in Regency Mall.

Store: Stewart's

Award Category: Merit — $50-100 million

Stewart's Fayette Mall ad reinforced Stewart's sophisticated style, a fashionable source for New York's discriminating tastes.

Store: Robinson's

Award Category: Merit — Best Institutional Newspaper

Robinson's sequential and comical "crowd stopping" ads announced the opening of their new store in Fort Myers, Florida. These attention-getting ads appeared over a period of several days teasing the customer into anticipating the store's opening.

Store: Macy's
Award Category: Second — Best
                    Institutional
                    Newspaper

Macy's combined merchandise availability and store opening festivities
in this traditional newspaper ad for
their new store in the Dallas
Galleria.

DISCOVER IT NOW. MACY'S

FIRST LEVEL

The Men's Store: the most noted names in design from traditional businesswear to trendsetting sportswear.

The Action Shop: sportswear collection for young men on the fast track.

Juniors: hot attitudes, energy and style in a never-changing environment. A world unto itself!

Women's Shoes: a whole wardrobe of looks to keep pace with your lifestyle.

Acccessories: the ultimate details! Designer handbags, belts, fine and fashion jewelry, sunglasses and much, much , more.

Beauty and Fragrance: cosmetics and treatment for men and women abound in our distinctive shops. And housed inside our elegant Parfumerie are the world's most coveted fragrance collections.

Macy's
us for
e on Ice
ficial
ting.
Betty
newest
loon!

ute of our
ade on ice!
the special
e dozens of
y celebrity
n parade:
Snoopy™,
Ann and
d Kickback
Pinky and
rite™ and
lus many
vorites. Lis-
White High

Wrap up the holidays with a gift for your elf.

AFTER CHRISTMAS SALE

SHOP FRIDAY 8:00 A.M.–10:00 P.M.

JOIN US TOMORROW AND TREAT YOURSELF TO THAT
SPECIAL SOMETHING YOU'VE BEEN EYEING ALL SEASON LONG—NOW
AT INCREDIBLE SAVINGS. YOU'LL FIND AN ABUNDANCE OF MERCHANDISE
THAT DIDN'T MAKE IT UNDER THE TREE. EVERYTHING FROM CLOTHES
TO SHOES TO GIFT ITEMS AND MORE. BUT HURRY IN. BECAUSE LIKE CHRISTMAS,
VALUES THIS GOOD COME ALONG BUT ONCE A YEAR. WE ARE CLOSED TODAY,
CHRISTMAS DAY.

nordstrom

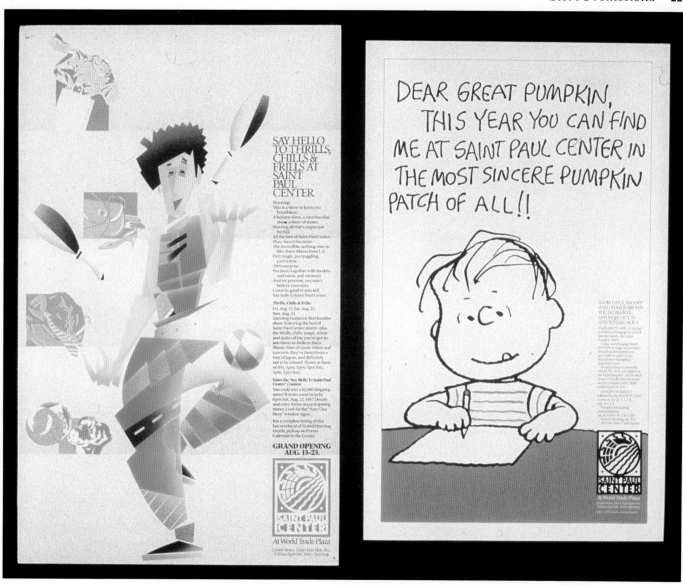

Store: St. Paul Center
Award Category: Second — Silver
Shopping Center

These St. Paul Center ads utilize a comical illustration and Linus of the Peanuts gang to announce the benefits of going to the mall.

Store: Nordstrom's
Award Category: Merit —
◄ Sale Ads

Nordstrom's promotes their after-Christmas sale with this "s"elf ad, suggesting that a special post holiday gift would be appropriate for you!

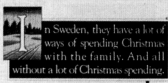

Store: IKEA
Award Category: Second — Silver
Institutional

IKEA lists several suggestions for a Swedish family Christmas. Reasonably-priced ornaments and decorations are displayed alongside directions for homemade crafts.

Store: Donaldson's
Award Category: Second — Silver
Institutional ➤

1965 World Series tickets were used as an inspiration to inspire the Minnesota Twins to victory in the 1987 World Series, in this boldface "encore" advertisement.

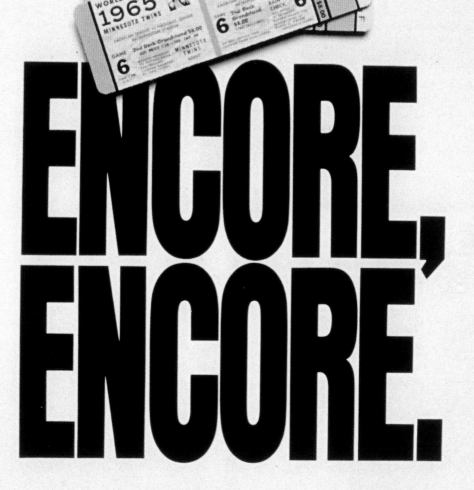

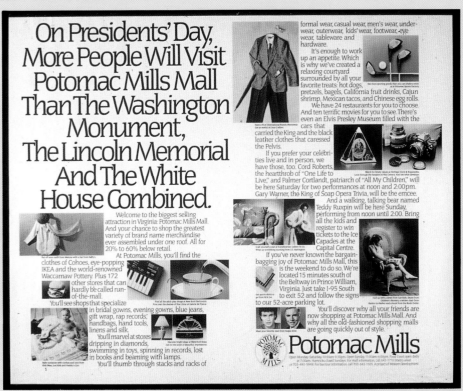

Potomac Mills proudly announces the vast number of people that will frequent their President's Day Sale in this collage type ad displaying a large assortment of available goods.

Creeds reminds its patrons of the versatility and convenience of having a Creeds credit card.

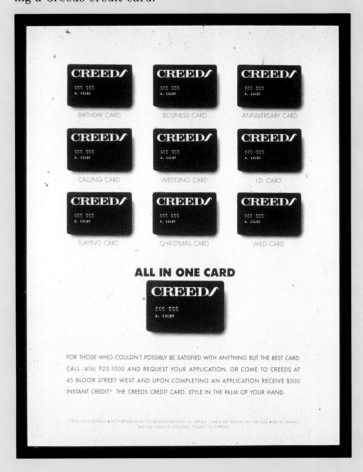

A glamorous model, clear photography, and a set of luggage launched the Portfolio campaign for Haywood Mall.

This Saturday, Please Join Us When We Tie The Knot.

August 8th at 10 am and 1 pm, come to our new Kenilworth Park store to learn everything there is to know about neckwear. You'll see a demonstration of how first-quality ties are made. And you'll get tips on proper bowtie and necktie selection and knotting. So be there. Or forever hold your peace.

J°S.A.Bank
Clothiers
Kenilworth Park, Towson

This Saturday, Find Out How To Dress For The Ball.

August 15th at 1:00 pm, drive on over to our new store at Kenilworth Park. We're having a fashion show highlighting the latest looks in J°S. A. Bank leisure wear. We want you to see how good you can look. Whether you're on a sandy beach or in a sandy trap.

J°S.A.Bank®
Clothiers
Kenilworth Park, Towson

Store: Jos. A. Bank Clothiers
Award Category: First — Gold
Campaigns Stores
$100-250 million

Jos. A. Bank Clothiers employed witty phrases and eye-catching photographic displays to create consumer awareness for the opening of several new stores.

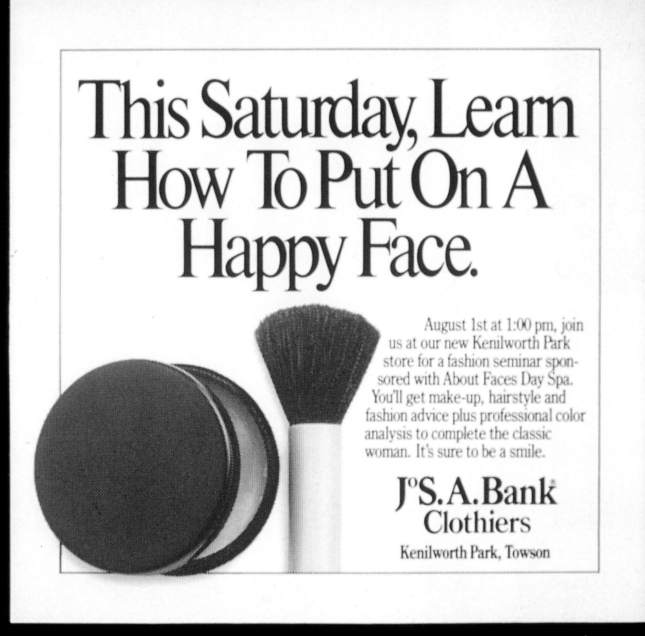

Store: Bamberger's
Award Category: Second — Best Institutional Newspaper

Bamberger's holiday Arcade hours and features were comically displayed in this colorful, clown-filled ad.

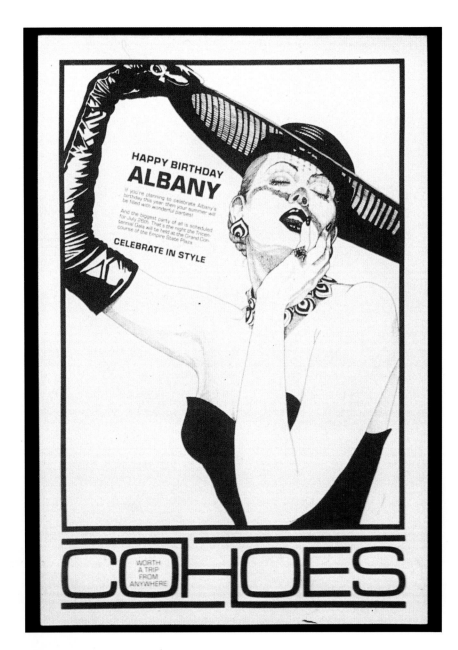

Store: Cohoes

Award Category: Merit — $5-25 million

Cohoes Empire State Plaza ad portrayed a glamour girl illustration to enhance their July 4th celebration theme at this excitement-filled shopping center in Albany.

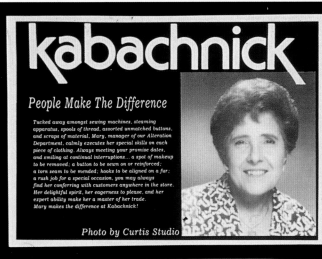

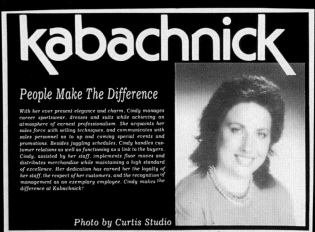

Store: Kabachnick
Award Category: Merit — Campaigns
                      Stores Under $5 million

Kabachnick stresses the importance of service with this real-life employee ad. Kabachnick's ad demonstrates that they care about their customers by showing their care for their employees.

Store: McCurdy's
Award Category: Second — $50-100 million

McCurdy's newspaper ad playfully enforces the merchandise availability and discount prices available at their summer sale.

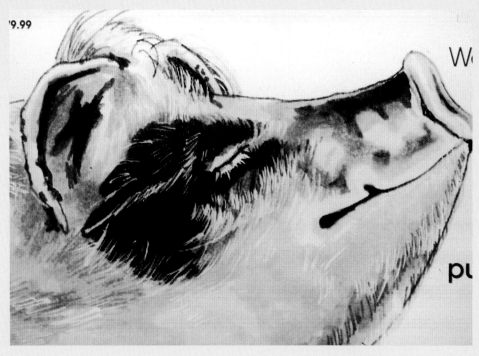

Store: Bockstruck's
Award Category: First — Under $5 million

Bockstruck's comically announces the opening of a new store with the use of these old time black and white photographs.
This crowd pleaser ad praised the features offered at the grand opening of a new Bockstruck's store.

Mrs. Reagan's luncheon will just have to wait!

The Grand Opening of Bockstruck's new store. It's worth planning your life around.

July 17, 18, 19 in the Galleria.

Bockstruck's
Fine Jewelers Since 1885

Get me out of that meeting with Spielberg next week!

The Grand Opening of Bockstruck's new store. It's worth planning your life around.

July 17, 18, 19 in the Galleria.

Bockstruck's
Fine Jewelers Since 1885

At Last Minneapolis, You've Got Your Bockstruck's Back!

Just when we'd gotten used to being in Minneapolis the past three years, our Nicollet Mall building was torn down last spring for a new construction project. So now we're at home in our newest home–the Galleria. Come renew old friendships (or start some new ones), during our Grand Opening Celebration.

Galleria Grand Opening Celebration: July 17-19
- **See a breathtaking, collector's 15-carat diamond** – and try it on for fun! Plus, an exclusive New York collection of 2 to 5 carat diamonds, at very special prices.
- **Magnificent trunk showing** of specially priced, period estate jewelry and dramatic one-of-a-kind designs from Boston's leading jewelry manufacturer.
- Music and complimentary refreshments.

Bockstruck's
Fine Jewelers Since 1885

Galleria in Edina • 70th and France • (612) 929-5165 • **St. Paul** • 27 W. 5th St. • (612) 222-1858

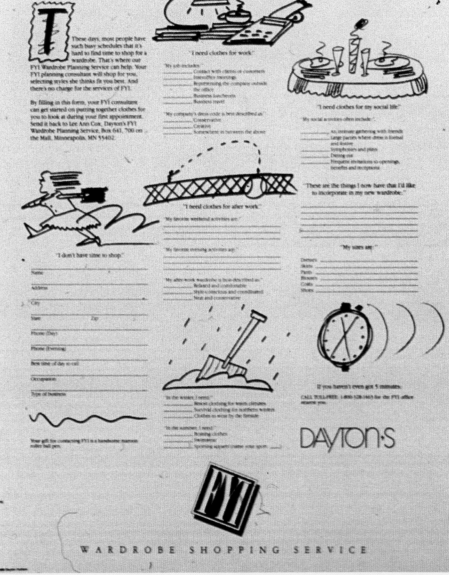

Store: Dayton Hudson
Award Category: Merit —
Institutional

Dayton Hudson employed this ad, a
direct mailer type, to introduce
their customers to the benefits of
their wardrobe shopping service.

Blouses
Coats
Shoes

If you haven't even got 5 minutes:

CALL TOLL-FREE: 1-800-328-1463 for the FYI off
nearest you.

"In the winter, I need:"
_____ Resort clothing for warm climates
_____ Survival clothing for northern winters
_____ Clothes to wear by the fireside

"In the summer, I need:"
_____ Boating clothes
_____ Swimwear
_____ Sporting apparel (name your sport _____)

DAYTON'S

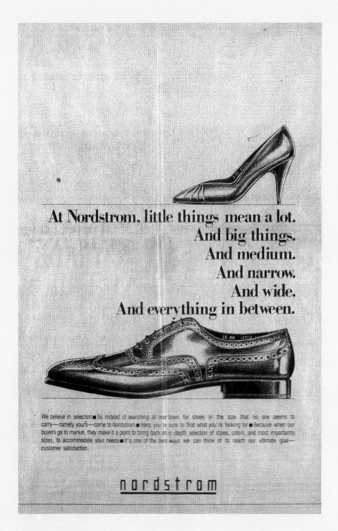

Store: Nordstrom's
Award Category: Merit —
                     Institutional

Nordstrom's white backdrop, bold typeface, and strategic word placement enhance this ad emphasizing the many characteristics of quality and comfort available at Nordstrom's.

Nordstrom's stresses "style" in this ad announcing a new store opening.

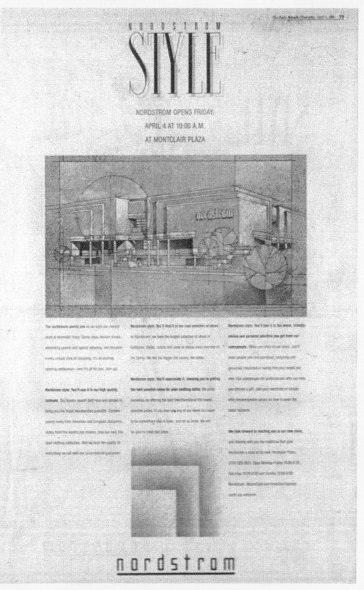

Store: Nordstrom's
Award Category: Merit —
                     Institutional

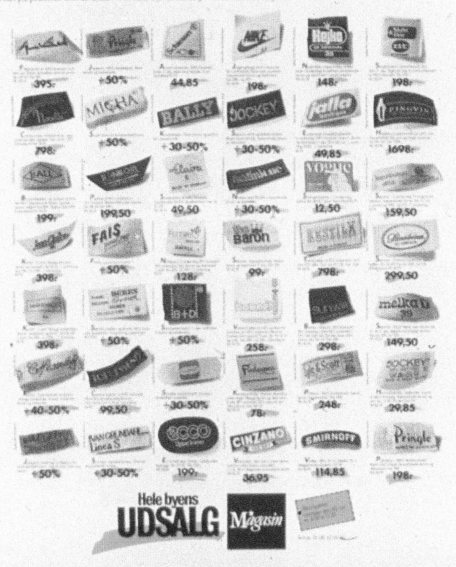

Store: Magasin du Nord

Award Category: Merit — Stores over $100 million

To display the various goods available to their shoppers, Magasin du Nord used this unique approach. Many people can easily identify what merchandise is being represented by recognition of the various logotypes. In this way, Magasin du Nord could display a number of items without having to clutter the page with too many product shots.

"Where do you think you are . . . Waldoff's?"

We don't mind that other stores think we're a pushover when it comes to returns.

You see, we feel that you should be happy about shopping at Waldoff's. We're confident enough in our commitment to quality, that we guarantee you can't buy anything at Waldoff's that you can't bring back!

In fact, we're only stubborn about one thing . . . your complete satisfaction.

That's why, should you need to make a return or exchange, you'll find our associates will serve you with the same attention and the same smiles as when you made your purchase . . . and that means with absolutely no hassle!

No one else guarantees your happiness like Waldoff's . . . proudly known as the "No Hassle Return" store!

WALDOFF'S

Store: Waldoff's
Award Category: Merit — Institutional Advertisement

Humorous black and white photography and blunt, straight forward copy portrays the customer-oriented philosophy of Waldoff's.

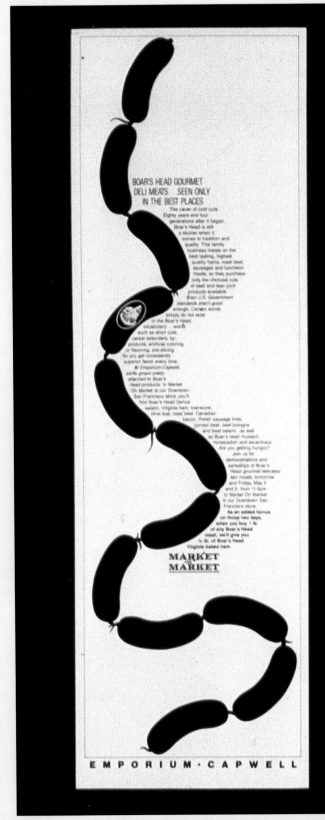

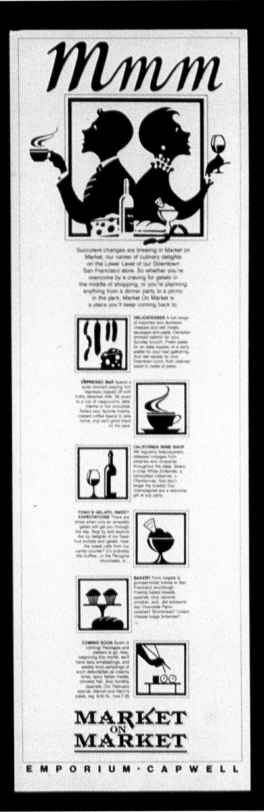

Store: Emporium Capwell

Award Category: Merit — Over $250 million

Emporium Capwell employed these silhouette/columnar ads to promote the gourmet foods and brand name deli meats, wines, espresso, and baked goods available at their "market on market" foodplace.

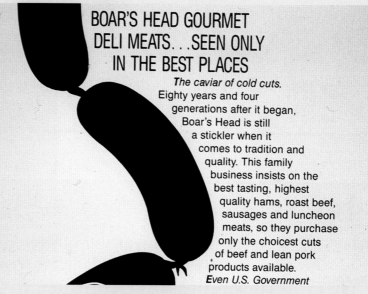

BOAR'S HEAD GOURMET DELI MEATS...SEEN ONLY IN THE BEST PLACES

The caviar of cold cuts. Eighty years and four generations after it began, Boar's Head is still a stickler when it comes to tradition and quality. This family business insists on the best tasting, highest quality hams, roast beef, sausages and luncheon meats, so they purchase only the choicest cuts of beef and lean pork products available. *Even U.S. Government*

ESPRESSO BAR Spend a quiet moment sipping rich espresso topped off with frothy steamed milk. Sit down to a cup of cappuccino, latté, mocha or hot chocolate. Select your favorite freshly-roasted coffee beans to take home, and we'll grind them on the spot.

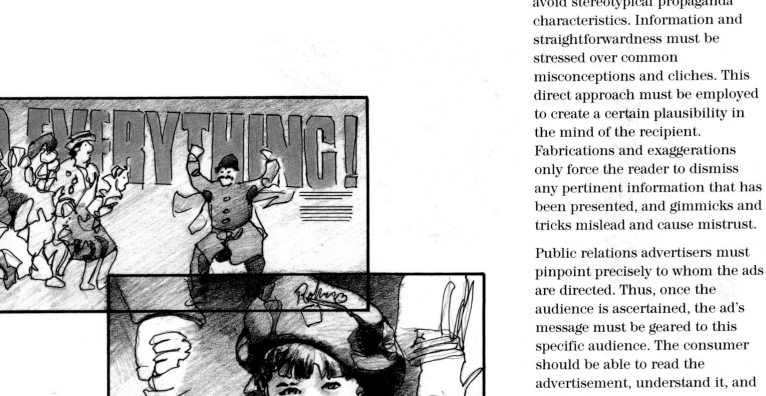

Public Relations advertising must avoid stereotypical propaganda characteristics. Information and straightforwardness must be stressed over common misconceptions and cliches. This direct approach must be employed to create a certain plausibility in the mind of the recipient. Fabrications and exaggerations only force the reader to dismiss any pertinent information that has been presented, and gimmicks and tricks mislead and cause mistrust.

Public relations advertisers must pinpoint precisely to whom the ads are directed. Thus, once the audience is ascertained, the ad's message must be geared to this specific audience. The consumer should be able to read the advertisement, understand it, and retain it.

Store: Sanger Harris
Award Category: Second — Institutional Advertisement

Sanger Harris' enthusiasm is stressed in this ad campaign revolving around the opening of a new store in the southwest United States. Descriptions of the southwest and points of interest further emphasize the store opening. This ad was done in conjunction with Southwest Airlines.

Store: Donaldson's
Award Category: First — Institutional

Donaldson's saluted the Centennial celebration of the Statue of Liberty with this ad.

Store: Carson Pirie Scott
Award Category: Special Award

Carson Pirie Scott's colorful ads
praised the availability of fashionable clothing, exciting activewear,
and attractive bed linens in Chicago.

Store: Racquet Sports
Award Category: First — Institutional
                    Advertisement

Overall physical fitness is the main thrust of Racquet Sports Group. Large playful headlines, folksy illustrations, and a "story" format copy inform the reader of this institution's health benefits.

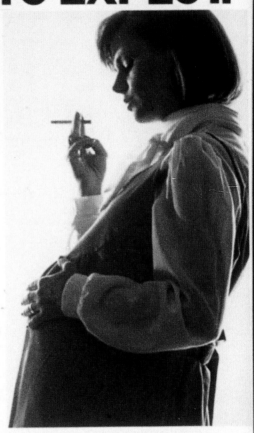

You know that smoking is bad for you. But if you're pregnant and smoke, your baby's health is at stake, too.

With every puff, you inhale 2,000 compounds. Of these, nicotine, carbon monoxide and benzo(a)pyrene are the most harmful. They can cross the placental barrier and affect the oxygen delivery to the developing fetus.

Ultimately, your smoking affects the length and weight of your baby and its ability to breathe correctly.

So quit smoking for your baby's sake. If you can't quit, cut down. Either way, it's one

Store: The Plain Dealer
Award Category: Merit — Public Service

The Plain Dealer's public service announcement offered straightforward facts on smoking and pregnancy. The simplicity of this ad fortifies its scare appeal.

Store: Raleigh's
Award Category: Merit — Institutional

Raleigh's bold typeface featuring "the Bay" promotes the benefits of the Ward Foundation in coordination with the Chesapeake Bay Foundation regarding culture and art forms.

Store: Dayton's
Award Category: Merit — Public Service
                    Ads

Dayton's utilized an illustrated
American flag to congratulate the
winner, Stars & Stripes, of the
Americas Cup.

Store: Dayton's
Award Category: First Prize — Gold/
                    Merchandise/$100–250
                    million

Dayton's and Rockport Shoes sponsored "A Walk for the Wild" event
that benefitted the Minnesota Zoo.
The ad briefly endorsed the shoes,
while introducing the benefits of
walking in this event in an informative, easy-to-understand manner.

A Walk For The Wild

Put on a pair of Rockport® walking shoes and go wild, Sunday, September 27, at the Minnesota Zoo

Rockport®, the pioneer in engineering footwear made
specifically for walking, is the first shoe manufacturer
to be awarded the Seal of Acceptance by the
American Podiatric Medical Association. Designed
to accommodate the unique walking motion of the foot,
Rockport® Shoes combine long-lasting materials for
support and   durability. So you know

The Kilter oxford for women ($60) | Women's Shoes.   they're   true walking shoes.

You'll find a wide variety of   styles in our
Men's and Women's Shoe Departments,   including these
shown. While you're there, be sure and   register for
"A Walk For The Wild." The two- and   five-mile walking
event at the Minnesota Zoo is   sponsored by
Rockport,® Dayton's, KARE-TV 11,   and Mpls./St. Paul
Magazine and will benefit the   "adopt an animal"
program of the Zoo.

Entry fee is $7 for adults 16 years and over; $4 for kids 15 and under. All
registrants will receive "A Walk For The Wild" t-shirt, and free admission to the
Zoo. When registering, simply designate which animal you would like to support:
dolphin, aviary exhibit,   wolves, snow monkey
or tiger.

Beginning at 12   noon, co-chairs Paul
Magers and Diana   Pierce from KARE-TV 11
will lead the pack in   the two- and five-mile walk,
which begins and ends   at the Zoo. After the walk,
enjoy a day of enter-   tainment, including
animal watching,   *The Supersport® for men ($72) | Men's Shoes.*   face painting,
clowns, music, awards, and a chance to win great prizes. And meet
Rob Sweetgall, the only man who has traveled the entire fifty United
States on foot, and author of "The Walker's Journal," Tuesday,
                         September 15, from 11 a.m.
                         to 12 noon in Women's
                         Shoes; and 12 noon to 1 p.m.
                         in Men's Shoes,
                         Downtown Minneapolis.
                         Receive a complimentary
                         copy of his book, while
                         supplies last.

DAYTON·S

TASTE ALL THE FLAVORS OF ART AT ARTPARK, HAPPY '86, AM&A'S

"*Stop looking through a keyhole and start looking at the sky.*"

at the vast blue
sky that is life.

Open the door. Say no to drugs!

Store: John Wannamaker
Award Category: First — Public
                   Service

John Wannamaker's direct anti-drug
ad simplistically, yet powerfully
states the facts about drug abuse.

Store: Carson Pirie Scott
Award Category: Special Award

Carson Pirie Scott's colorful ads praised the availability of fashionable clothing, exciting activewear, and attractive bed linens in Chicago.

STORES